The Lazy Entrepreneur:

101 Passive Income Ideas That Anyone Can Do

By Alexander J. Kelley

The Lazy Entrepreneur: 101 Passive Income Ideas That Anyone Can Do
Copyright © 2023 by Alexander J. Kelley

Book Cover by Alexander J. Kelley

First Edition 2003

www.alexanderkelley.com

To my mother, Vivian.
The cornerstone of our family, making countless sacrifices for us kids, planting the seed for us to strive to find innovative ways to make extra money. We love you.

Introduction

Welcome to "The Lazy Investor: 101 Passive Income Ideas Anyone Can Do." If you're looking for a book that will teach you how to make money without putting in too much effort, then you're in the right place.

The idea of making money while lounging on the couch or taking a vacation might sound too good to be true, but it's not. With the right strategies, anyone can generate passive income streams that provide financial security and independence.

This book is designed to be a guide to the world of passive income, from the basics of what it is and how it works, to a detailed breakdown of 101 different ways to make passive income. Whether you're a student, a stay-at-home parent, a retiree, or just someone looking to diversify your income streams, this book will give you the tools and ideas you need to achieve your financial goals.

Throughout this book, we'll explore a variety of strategies and techniques for generating passive income, from investing in stocks and real estate to creating digital products and building online businesses. We'll also look at some of the pros and cons of each approach, so you can make informed decisions about which strategies are right for you.

Above all, this book is about empowering you to take control of your financial future. By learning about the different methods with which you can generate passive income, you'll be able to create a more stable and prosperous future for yourself and your loved ones. So, let's get started on this exciting journey together.

Table of Contents

Chapter 1: Real Estate

Rental Properties

Rental properties are a popular way to generate passive income. This involves purchasing a property, such as an apartment, condo, or house, and then renting it out to tenants. The rent paid by tenants provides a steady stream of income for the property owner.

To generate passive income through rental properties, there are a few key steps to follow:

1. *Purchase the property*: The first step is to purchase a property that is suitable for renting out. This could involve researching the local real estate market to find a property that is in a desirable location and has a high rental demand.
2. *Prepare the property for rent*: Once the property is purchased, it may require some preparation before it can be rented out. This could involve making any necessary repairs, cleaning the property, and ensuring that it meets local housing codes.
3. *Find tenants*: The next step is to find tenants to rent out the property. This could involve advertising the property on rental websites, working with a property management company, or using a real estate agent to find tenants.
4. *Manage the property*: Once tenants are in place, the property owner will need to manage the property. This could involve collecting rent, responding to tenant requests or complaints, and maintaining the property. If this sounds like too much to handle, you can explore hiring a management company to handle this for you, in exchange for their monthly fee.
5. *Generate passive income*: Finally, rental income will start coming in, providing a passive income stream for the property owner.

If you're considering rental properties for passive income, here are some things to be aware of:

1. *Initial investment*: Rental properties require an initial investment to purchase the property, make any necessary repairs or renovations, and furnish the property if needed. Be aware of the

initial investment required and ensure that it aligns with your financial goals.

2. **Ongoing expenses**: Rental properties also come with ongoing expenses such as mortgage payments, property taxes, insurance, maintenance, and repair costs. Be aware of the ongoing expenses and ensure that they're factored into your financial plan.

3. **Rental market**: The rental market can vary by location, with some areas having a high demand for rental properties while others have a low demand. Be aware of the rental market in the area where you're considering purchasing a rental property and ensure that it aligns with your financial goals.

4. **Tenant screening**: Screening potential tenants is an important aspect of renting out a property, as it can help to ensure that you have reliable and responsible tenants. Be aware of the tenant screening process and ensure that it's thorough and legally compliant.

5. **Landlord-tenant laws**: Familiarize yourself with the landlord-tenant laws in your area, as these laws can vary by location and can impact your rights and responsibilities as a landlord.

6. **Property management**: Property management can be time-consuming and may require a significant amount of effort. Be aware of the time commitment involved and consider hiring a property management company if you're unable or unwilling to manage the property yourself.

7. **Income potential**: Rental properties can provide a reliable source of passive income, but the potential earnings can vary depending on factors such as the rental market, location, and ongoing expenses. Be realistic about the potential earnings and ensure that they align with your financial goals.

The amount of money you can expect to make on rental properties for passive income can vary widely depending on several factors such as the location, type of property, rental rates, occupancy rates, and expenses such as property taxes, maintenance, and mortgage payments.

On average, rental property owners can expect to earn around 6-10% of the property value per year in rental income. For example, if you purchase a rental property for $300,000, you might expect to earn around $18,000 to $30,000 per year in rental income.

However, it's important to note that the actual rental income can vary depending on several factors such as the local rental market, competition, and the quality of the property. Additionally, expenses such as property taxes, maintenance, and mortgage payments can also significantly impact your net income.

While owning and managing rental properties can be a lot of work, it can also provide a stable source of passive income over the long term. With the right property in the right location and good management practices, rental properties can be a successful way to generate passive income.

House Flipping

House flipping is a popular method for generating passive income through real estate investment. This involves purchasing a property, typically a run-down or distressed property, and renovating it to increase its value before selling it for a profit. The goal is to buy low, improve the property, and then sell high.

Here are the steps involved in generating passive income through house flipping:

1. *Find a suitable property*: The first step is to find a property that has potential for renovation and resale. This could involve researching the local real estate market to identify undervalued properties or working with a real estate agent who specializes in house flipping.
2. *Purchase the property*: Once a suitable property is identified, the next step is to purchase it. This may involve financing the purchase through a mortgage or using cash to buy the property outright.
3. *Renovate the property*: After purchasing the property, the next step is to renovate it to increase its value. This could involve making structural repairs, updating the kitchen and bathrooms, replacing flooring or fixtures, and landscaping.
4. *Sell the property*: Once the property has been renovated, it can be put on the market for sale. The goal is to sell the property for a higher price than what was paid for it, including the cost of renovations.
5. *Repeat the process*: After selling the property, the profits can be reinvested into purchasing and renovating another property, repeating the process to generate additional passive income.

If you're considering house flipping for passive income, here are some things to be aware of:

1. *Real estate market*: The real estate market can be unpredictable and can impact the success of your house flipping project. Be

aware of the current market conditions and ensure that you're purchasing a property at a reasonable price.

2. ***Initial investment***: House flipping requires an initial investment to purchase the property and make any necessary repairs or renovations. Be aware of the initial investment required and ensure that it aligns with your financial goals.

3. ***Time commitment***: House flipping can be time-consuming and may require a significant amount of effort. Be aware of the time commitment involved and ensure that it aligns with your schedule and other obligations.

4. ***Renovation costs***: Renovating a property can be expensive, and unexpected costs can arise. Be aware of the renovation costs and ensure that they're factored into your financial plan.

5. ***Legal requirements***: Flipping a house may require certain legal requirements, such as obtaining permits and complying with building codes. Be aware of the legal requirements in your area and ensure that you're compliant.

6. ***Selling the property***: Selling the property can be challenging, and the price you're able to sell it for can impact the success of your house flipping project. Be aware of the selling process and ensure that you're pricing the property appropriately.

7. ***Risks***: House flipping involves financial risks, such as the possibility of the property not selling for the desired price or not selling at all. Be aware of the risks involved and ensure that you're comfortable with them before investing in a house flipping project.

On average, house flippers can earn a profit of around 10-20% of the property value, although this can vary widely depending on the specific circumstances of the property and the market conditions. For example, if you purchase a property for $200,000 and invest $50,000 in renovations, you might expect to sell the property for around $300,000 and earn a profit of $50,000 to $100,000.

If flipping houses interests you as a possible passive income option, there are several resources you can turn to for information and guidance. Here are some options:

1. ***Books***: There are many books available about flipping houses, ranging from basic guides to in-depth analysis of the market. Some popular titles include ***"The Book on Flipping Houses" by J. Scott, "Flip: How to Find, Fix, and Sell Houses for Profit" by Rick Villani and Clay Davis,*** and ***"The Flipping Blueprint" by Luke Weber***.
2. ***Online courses***: Many real estate investors offer online courses on flipping houses, often including step-by-step instructions and access to support networks. Some popular options include courses from ***FortuneBuilders***, ***House Flipping School***, and the ***Real Estate Institute***.
3. ***Real estate seminars***: Attending a real estate seminar can be a great way to learn about flipping houses from experts in the field. Some seminars focus specifically on flipping houses, while others cover a broader range of real estate topics.
4. ***Networking***: Networking with other real estate investors can provide valuable insights and connections. Consider joining a local real estate investing group or attending real estate conferences to meet like-minded individuals.
5. ***Online resources***: There are many online resources available for those interested in flipping houses, including blogs, forums, and social media groups. Some popular options include ***BiggerPockets***, ***FlippingJunkie***, and ***REtipster***.

While house flipping can require a significant amount of work and effort, the potential for profit is high, making it an attractive option for generating passive income through real estate investment. By following a well-planned strategy, house flipping can be a successful way to generate long-term, sustainable passive income.

Airbnb Rentals

Airbnb rentals are a popular way to generate passive income through real estate investment. This involves renting out a property, typically a vacation rental, on Airbnb for short-term stays. The income is generated through the nightly rental rates paid by guests, with the property owner receiving a portion of the fee as payment.

Here are the steps involved in generating passive income through Airbnb rentals:

1. *Find a suitable property*: The first step is to find a property that is suitable for renting out on Airbnb. This could be a vacation home, a spare room in your house, or a separate apartment or rental property.
2. *Prepare the property for rent*: Once the property is identified, it may require some preparation before it can be rented out on Airbnb. This could involve making any necessary repairs, cleaning the property, and ensuring that it meets local housing codes.
3. *List the property on Airbnb*: After the property is prepared for rent, it can be listed on Airbnb for short-term stays. The property owner can set the rental rates and availability and communicate with potential guests through the Airbnb platform.
4. *Manage the property*: Once guests are in place, the property owner will need to manage the property. This could involve responding to guest requests or complaints, coordinating check-ins and check-outs, and maintaining the property. If this sounds like too much to handle, you can explore hiring a management company to handle this for you, in exchange for their monthly fee.
5. *Generate passive income*: Finally, rental income will start coming in, providing a passive income stream for the property owner.

If you're looking for alternatives to Airbnb for renting out your property, here are some options to consider:

1. *Vrbo*: Vrbo is a vacation rental platform that allows property owners to list their homes, apartments, and other properties for rent

to vacationers. Like Airbnb, Vrbo offers a range of tools and resources to help property owners manage their listings, communicate with guests, and accept bookings.

2. *HomeAway*: HomeAway is another vacation rental platform that offers similar features and functionality to Vrbo. HomeAway is particularly popular with property owners who want to rent out their homes or vacation properties for longer periods of time, such as several weeks or months.

3. *FlipKey*: FlipKey is a vacation rental platform that is owned by TripAdvisor. Like Airbnb, FlipKey allows property owners to list their homes, apartments, and other properties for rent to travelers. FlipKey offers a range of tools and resources to help property owners manage their listings and communicate with guests.

4. *Booking.com*: While Booking.com is primarily known as a hotel booking platform, it also offers a range of alternative accommodations, including vacation rentals, apartments, and guesthouses. Property owners can list their properties on Booking.com and receive bookings from travelers from around the world.

5. *OneFineStay*: OneFineStay is a luxury vacation rental platform that focuses on high-end properties in major cities around the world. Property owners can list their luxury homes or apartments on OneFineStay and receive bookings from discerning travelers who are looking for a more exclusive experience.

If you're considering renting out your property on Airbnb for passive income, here are some things to be aware of:

1. *Local regulations*: Regulations around short-term rentals can vary widely depending on the location. Make sure you understand any local laws and regulations around short-term rentals in your area before listing your property on Airbnb.

2. *Insurance*: Make sure you have the appropriate insurance coverage for short-term rentals, as your regular homeowner's insurance may not cover any damages or liabilities associated with hosting guests.

3. *Guest screening*: As a host, you can screen potential guests before accepting a reservation. Make sure to carefully review any guest profiles, past reviews, and communication with potential guests to ensure they are a good fit for your property.
4. *Cleaning and maintenance*: Hosting guests on Airbnb requires regular cleaning and maintenance of your property. Make sure you have a plan in place for cleaning and upkeep to ensure your property is always in top condition for guests.
5. *Communication*: Good communication is key to providing a positive guest experience. Make sure you are responsive to guest inquiries and questions and provide clear and detailed information about your property and the surrounding area.
6. *Pricing*: Setting the right price for your listing can be tricky. Research comparable properties in your area and consider factors such as seasonality, local events, and demand to determine the best pricing strategy for your property.
7. *Guest satisfaction*: The success of your Airbnb listing depends on positive guest reviews and ratings. Make sure you provide a comfortable and enjoyable experience for your guests to ensure positive reviews and repeat bookings.

On average, Airbnb hosts can expect to earn around $924 per month, according to data from *Airdna*. However, the actual rental income can vary widely depending on several factors such as the local rental market, competition, and the quality and location of the property. Hosts can earn significantly more than the average, especially if they are in a high-demand area or offer unique amenities or experiences. A luxurious beachfront property or a trendy downtown apartment can command significantly higher rental rates.

It's important to note that there are expenses associated with Airbnb rentals, such as cleaning fees, property management fees, and taxes. There may be legal requirements or restrictions on short-term rentals in your area, so it's important to research and comply with any regulations before listing your property on Airbnb.

While managing an Airbnb rental property can require some effort, it can also provide a stable source of passive income over the long term.

Storage Space Rentals

Renting out storage space is a great way to generate passive income. Here are the steps involved in generating passive income through storage space rentals:

1. ***Find a suitable storage space***: The first step is to find a suitable storage space that is available for rent. This could be a self-storage facility, a garage, or a spare room in your house.
2. ***Prepare the storage space for rent***: Once you have identified a suitable storage space, it may require some preparation before it can be rented out. This could involve cleaning the space, making any necessary repairs, and ensuring that it is secure and protected from weather and other potential hazards.
3. ***List the storage space for rent***: After the storage space is prepared for rent, it can be listed on various platforms that allow you to advertise your storage space. These platforms may include online marketplaces like ***SpareFoot*** and ***Neighbor***, or local classified ads and community bulletin boards.
4. ***Manage the storage space***: Once renters are in place, you will need to manage the storage space. This could involve communicating with renters, collecting rent payments, and ensuring that the space is kept clean and secure.
5. ***Generate passive income***: Finally, rental income will start coming in, providing a passive income stream for the storage space owner.

On average, storage unit owners can expect to earn around $0.75 to $1.50 per square foot per month in rental income. For example, if you have a 100 square foot storage unit, you might expect to earn around $75 to $150 per month in rental income.

However, the actual rental income can vary depending on several factors such as the local rental market, competition, and the quality of the storage facility. Additionally, expenses such as property taxes, maintenance, and insurance can also significantly impact your net income.

While managing a storage space rental can require some effort, it can also provide a stable source of passive income over the long term. With the right location and good management practices, storage space rentals can be a successful way to generate passive income. Additionally, the demand for storage space is always present, making it a viable option for those looking to generate passive income in the real estate market.

REITs (Real Estate Investment Trusts)

Real Estate Investment Trusts, or REITs, are a popular way for investors to generate passive income through real estate. Here are the steps involved in generating passive income through REITs:

1. ***Invest in a REIT***: The first step is to invest in a REIT, which is a type of investment fund that owns and operates income-generating real estate properties. REITs can be publicly traded on stock exchanges, making it easy for investors to buy and sell shares.
2. ***Receive distributions***: As a REIT shareholder, you will receive regular distributions from the rental income generated by the properties owned by the REIT. These distributions are typically made on a quarterly basis and can provide a stable source of passive income.
3. ***Reinvest distributions***: Many REITs offer the option to reinvest distributions, which allows investors to purchase additional shares of the REIT without incurring additional costs. Reinvesting distributions can help investors to increase their ownership stake in the REIT and generate even more passive income over time.
4. ***Monitor the performance of the REIT***: While REITs can be a great way to generate passive income, it's important to monitor the performance of the REIT over time. This includes tracking the rental income generated by the properties owned by the REIT, as well as the overall performance of the real estate market.

There are many reputable REITs available for investors to invest in. Here are some sources for finding reputable REITs:

1. ***Public stock exchanges***: Many REITs are publicly traded on stock exchanges such as the ***New York Stock Exchange (NYSE)*** and ***NASDAQ***. Investors can find REITs by searching for them on stock exchange websites and can easily invest in them through a brokerage account.
2. ***REIT-focused mutual funds and exchange-traded funds (ETFs)***: Some mutual funds and ETFs focus specifically on investing in

REITs. These funds typically hold a diversified portfolio of REITs and offer investors exposure to the real estate market.

3. *Investment research websites*: There are many investment research websites, such as *Morningstar* and *Seeking Alpha*, that provide analysis and ratings of different REITs. These websites can help investors to identify reputable REITs that align with their investment goals and risk tolerance.

4. *Financial advisors*: Investors can also consult with a financial advisor to help them identify reputable REITs and other investment opportunities. Financial advisors can provide personalized advice based on an investor's financial goals, risk tolerance, and investment timeline.

When looking for reputable REITs, it's important to conduct due diligence and research the REIT's history, management team, portfolio of properties, and financial performance. Additionally, investors should pay attention to the REIT's dividend yield, which is the percentage of income paid out to shareholders in the form of dividends, as this is a key factor in generating passive income through REITs.

Real Estate Investment Trusts (REITs) can provide a passive income stream for investors, but there are some things to be aware of before investing:

1. *Understand the investment*: REITs are a way to invest in real estate without owning physical property. They allow investors to purchase shares in a portfolio of properties, which generates rental income and potentially capital gains. Before investing, it's important to understand the investment strategy, management team, and financials of the REIT.

2. *Risk*: While REITs can provide a stable income stream, they are not risk-free. REITs can be affected by changes in interest rates, economic conditions, and tenant vacancies. It's important to understand the risks associated with the specific REIT and the real estate market in general.

3. *Fees*: REITs can have various fees associated with them, such as management fees and performance fees. Make sure to read the

prospectus carefully to understand all fees associated with the investment.

4. **Dividend payments**: REITs are required to distribute at least 90% of their taxable income to shareholders as dividends. However, the dividend yield can vary widely between different REITs, and there is no guarantee that the dividend payment will remain stable or increase over time.

5. **Diversification**: As with any investment, it's important to diversify your portfolio. Investing in multiple REITs, as well as other asset classes, can help spread out risk and potentially increase returns over time.

6. **Tax considerations**: REITs have specific tax considerations, and it's important to understand how the investment will affect your tax situation.

On average, REITs can offer dividend yields ranging from around 3% to 6%, although some REITs may offer higher or lower yields depending on the specific circumstances. For example, a REIT that invests in high-end office buildings in a prime location may offer a lower yield than a REIT that invests in low-cost apartment complexes in a less desirable area.

However, it's important to note that the value of your investment in a REIT can fluctuate based on market conditions and other factors. Additionally, REITs are subject to fees and expenses, such as management fees, that can impact your net return.

By investing in a REIT, investors can generate passive income from real estate without the hassle of owning and managing individual properties. Additionally, REITs offer the potential for diversification, as they typically own a portfolio of different types of properties across multiple geographic locations. Overall, REITs can be a great way to generate passive income for investors who are interested in the real estate market.

Commercial Property Rentals

Commercial property rentals can be an excellent source of passive income for investors who are interested in the real estate market. Here are the steps involved in generating passive income through commercial property rentals:

1. *Invest in commercial real estate*: The first step is to invest in commercial real estate by purchasing a property or investing in a real estate partnership. Commercial properties can include office buildings, retail space, warehouses, and more.
2. *Find tenants*: Once you own a commercial property, the next step is to find tenants to rent out the space. This can involve advertising the property, working with a broker, or using a property management company to find and vet potential tenants.
3. *Collect rent*: As a commercial property owner, you will receive regular rent payments from your tenants. This rent can provide a stable source of passive income over time.
4. *Manage the property*: While commercial property rentals can generate passive income, it's important to note that owning and managing a commercial property can require some level of active involvement. This can include overseeing repairs and maintenance, responding to tenant needs and concerns, and ensuring that the property follows local regulations.
5. *Monitor the market*: It's important to monitor the commercial real estate market over time to ensure that your property remains competitive and in demand. This can involve tracking market trends, staying up to date on local zoning and regulatory changes, and staying informed about new developments and construction projects in the area.

Here are some of the best places to find available commercial properties:

1. *Commercial real estate brokers*: Commercial real estate brokers specialize in helping buyers and sellers of commercial properties. They can provide valuable insight into the local market, help

buyers find properties that meet their specific needs, and negotiate deals on their behalf.

2. ***Online listing platforms***: There are several online listing platforms that specialize in commercial real estate listings. Examples include ***LoopNet***, ***CommercialCafe***, and ***CoStar***. These platforms allow users to search for available properties based on location, property type, and other criteria.

3. ***Auctions***: Commercial properties may be sold through public auctions. These auctions can be found through online platforms like ***Auction.com*** and ***Real Estate Auctions***, or through local auction houses.

4. ***Government agencies***: Some commercial properties may be owned by government agencies or sold through public auctions. Buyers can check with local and state governments to find out about available properties.

5. ***Networking***: Networking with other real estate investors and professionals can be a valuable way to learn about available commercial properties. Attending industry events and conferences, joining real estate investment clubs, and connecting with other professionals on social media platforms can all help investors find potential investment opportunities.

When searching for commercial properties, it's important to conduct thorough due diligence and research to ensure that the property meets your investment goals and criteria. This may include reviewing financial statements, inspecting the property, researching local zoning and regulations, and evaluating the local market.

Commercial rental properties can be a great source of passive income, but there are some things to be aware of before investing:

1. ***Location***: Location is a key factor in the success of a commercial rental property. Make sure to research the local market and choose a property in a desirable location with strong demand from tenants.

2. ***Property type***: Commercial properties can include office buildings, retail spaces, industrial warehouses, and more. It's important to choose a property type that fits your investment goals and matches the local market demand.

3. **Tenant quality**: The quality of tenants can impact the stability of rental income. Make sure to carefully screen potential tenants and choose those with a strong credit history and stable business operations.
4. **Property management**: Managing a commercial rental property can be time-consuming and require specialized knowledge. Consider hiring a professional property management company to handle maintenance, tenant relations, and other tasks.
5. **Financing**: Commercial properties can require significant financing and obtaining a loan can be more difficult than with residential properties. Make sure to have a solid financial plan in place and understand the financing options available.
6. **Market conditions**: Commercial rental properties can be impacted by changes in the local economy, interest rates, and other market conditions. Make sure to stay up to date on market trends and adjust your investment strategy accordingly.
7. **Legal considerations**: Commercial rental properties are subject to different regulations and legal requirements than residential properties. Make sure to consult with a lawyer to ensure compliance with local laws and regulations.

On average, commercial property owners can expect to earn around 6% to 12% of the property value per year in rental income. For example, if you have a commercial property worth $1 million, you might expect to earn around $60,000 to $120,000 per year in rental income.

The actual rental income can vary depending on several factors such as the local rental market, competition, and the quality of the property. Expenses such as property taxes, maintenance, and insurance can also significantly impact your net income.

By investing in commercial property rentals, investors can generate passive income from a diversified portfolio of properties. Commercial properties can offer the potential for higher rental income than residential properties, however, it's important to note that commercial property rentals require active management and involvement. It may not be suitable for all investors. One option may be to outsource management to a firm.

Raw Land Investments

Raw land investments can be a great way to generate passive income for investors. Unlike other types of real estate investments that require active management and maintenance, raw land investments can be relatively hands-off. With raw land, investors have the option to hold onto the property for the long-term and potentially realize significant appreciation, or they can develop the land for various uses such as agriculture, residential or commercial development, or even recreational purposes.

Raw land investments can generate passive income in several ways, including:

1. *Leasing for agriculture or livestock*: One way to generate passive income from raw land is to lease it to farmers or ranchers for agricultural or livestock use. This allows landowners to earn income without having to actively manage the land.
2. *Leasing for hunting or recreational use*: Raw land can also be leased to hunters or outdoor enthusiasts for recreational use. This can be a profitable way to generate passive income, particularly for land located near popular hunting or fishing destinations.
3. *Timber harvesting*: Raw land that contains timber can be leased or sold to logging companies for harvesting. This can be a profitable way to generate passive income, particularly if the land is in a region with high demand for timber.
4. *Mineral rights*: Raw land that contains mineral rights can be leased or sold to mining companies for extraction. This can be a highly profitable way to generate passive income, particularly if the land is in a region with valuable minerals.
5. *Development potential*: Raw land can also be held for future development potential. This can be a long-term strategy for generating passive income, as the land appreciates in value over time.

Finding raw land investments can be challenging, but here are some strategies to consider:

1. *Real estate websites*: Real estate websites such as *Zillow*, *Realtor.com*, and *LandWatch* list raw land for sale across the United States. You can use these websites to search for raw land investments based on location, price, and other criteria.
2. *Auctions*: Some raw land investments may be sold through public auctions. You can search for upcoming auctions online or through local auction houses.
3. *Direct mail campaigns*: Some investors have had success finding raw land investments by sending direct mail campaigns to landowners in targeted areas. These campaigns may include letters or postcards expressing interest in purchasing raw land.
4. *Local real estate agents*: Local real estate agents may have information on raw land for sale in their area. They can also provide valuable insight into the local market and help investors identify potential investment opportunities.
5. *Online land marketplaces*: Online land marketplaces such as *Land.com* and *LandHub* specialize in connecting buyers and sellers of raw land. You can use these websites to search for raw land investments based on location, price, and other criteria.

Raw land investments can be a unique source of passive income, but there are some things to be aware of before investing:

1. *Location*: The location of the land can greatly impact its value and potential for income. Make sure to research the local market and choose a property in a desirable location with strong potential for future development or use.
2. *Zoning and regulations*: Raw land is subject to local zoning and land use regulations. Make sure to research these regulations before investing to ensure that the land can be used for your intended purpose.
3. *Development costs*: If you plan to develop the land for income-generating purposes, make sure to factor in the costs of development, such as grading, utilities, and permits.
4. *Income potential*: Raw land may not generate immediate income, so it's important to have a long-term plan for income generation.

This could include leasing the land for agriculture or other uses, or waiting for the value of the land to increase for eventual sale.

5. *Environmental considerations*: Raw land may have environmental issues such as wetlands or endangered species habitats. Make sure to conduct environmental assessments and obtain any necessary permits before making an investment.

6. *Access and easements*: Access to the land and any easements for utility or other purposes can impact the value and development potential of the land. Make sure to research and obtain any necessary easements before investing.

7. *Legal considerations*: Raw land investments are subject to legal considerations such as property taxes, liens, and title issues. Make sure to conduct a thorough title search and consult with a lawyer to ensure that the investment is legally sound.

Grazing land rental rates can range from $10 to $50 per acre per month, depending on the location, quality, and availability of the land. If you have a large amount of land and can lease it out for grazing, you could potentially generate significant passive income.

Hunting lease rates can range from $10 to $40 per acre per year, depending on the location, quality, and availability of the land, as well as the type of hunting allowed. Additionally, recreational lease rates can vary widely depending on the type of activities allowed, such as camping, hiking, or fishing.

Timber lease rates can range from $10 to $100 per acre per year, depending on the location, quality, and availability of the timber, as well as the prevailing market prices for timber.

When investing in raw land, it's important to conduct thorough due diligence and research to ensure that the land meets your investment goals and criteria. This may include evaluating the land's location, accessibility, zoning and land use regulations, environmental concerns, and potential income streams. By taking the time to carefully research potential raw land investments, investors can make informed investment decisions and generate passive income over the long term.

Mobile Home Parks

Mobile home parks can generate passive income for investors in several ways, including:

1. *Lot rental income*: The primary way that mobile home parks generate income is through lot rental fees. Tenants typically own their mobile homes but rent the land from the park owner. This allows investors to generate a steady stream of passive income from lot rental fees.
2. *Amenities*: Mobile home parks can offer amenities such as laundry facilities, playgrounds, and community centers, which can generate additional income for the park owner. Amenities can be an attractive selling point for potential tenants and can help to increase occupancy rates and rental fees.
3. *Upside potential*: Mobile home parks can offer significant upside potential for investors. By improving the park's amenities, raising rents, or adding new lots, investors can increase the park's cash flow and generate higher returns.
4. *Lower maintenance costs*: Mobile home parks can have lower maintenance costs than other types of real estate investments. Tenants are responsible for maintaining their own homes, which can reduce the park owner's maintenance costs.
5. *High demand*: Mobile homes can be an affordable housing option for many people, which can lead to high demand for mobile home park rentals. This can help to ensure a steady stream of rental income for park owners.

To generate passive income from mobile home parks, investors can purchase an existing park or develop a new one. Investing in an existing park may require less upfront capital but may also come with the risk of inheriting any existing problems or issues. Developing a new park may require more upfront capital but offers the opportunity to build a park that meets specific needs and can be designed for maximum efficiency and profitability.

There are several ways to find existing mobile home parks available for sale:

1. *Online listing platforms*: There are several online listing platforms that specialize in commercial real estate listings, including mobile home parks. Examples include *LoopNet*, *MobileHomeParkStore*, and *MHBay*.
2. *Real estate agents*: Commercial real estate agents may have listings for mobile home parks for sale in their local area. Consider reaching out to a few agents who specialize in commercial real estate in your desired location.
3. *Industry publications*: There are several industry publications that focus on mobile home parks and manufactured housing, such as *Mobile Home Park Magazine* and *Manufactured Housing Review*. These publications often include listings of mobile home parks for sale.
4. *Auctions*: Mobile home parks may occasionally be sold at auction, either online or in-person. Check with local auction houses to see if they have any upcoming sales that include mobile home parks.

When looking for an existing mobile home park to purchase, it's important to do your due diligence and thoroughly research the property and its financials before making an offer. Consider working with a real estate attorney and a financial advisor to ensure that you're making a sound investment.

Building a mobile home park from scratch can be a complex and involved process, but here are some general steps to consider:

1. *Research local zoning and land use regulations*: Before investing in creating a mobile home park, it's important to research local zoning and land use regulations. Some areas may prohibit mobile home parks or have strict regulations governing their development and operation.
2. *Find a suitable location*: Once you have determined that it's possible to create a mobile home park in your area, you'll need to find a suitable location for the park. Look for areas that have high

demand for affordable housing and that are easily accessible by roads.

3. ***Secure financing***: Creating a mobile home park can be expensive, so it's important to secure financing before beginning the development process. Consider working with a lender that specializes in mobile home park financing.

4. ***Develop the infrastructure***: To create a mobile home park, you'll need to develop the necessary infrastructure, including roads, utility connections, and other amenities. This can be a significant expense, so it's important to budget accordingly.

5. ***Obtain necessary permits and approvals***: Before you can begin renting out mobile home lots, you'll need to obtain necessary permits and approvals from local government agencies. This may include zoning permits, building permits, and environmental permits.

6. ***Market the park***: Once the park is ready for tenants, you'll need to market it to potential renters. Consider working with local real estate agents, advertising online, and offering move-in incentives to attract renters.

In general, mobile home park rental rates can range from $200 to $500 per month per home, depending on the location, quality, and amenities offered in the park. The average monthly lot rent for a mobile home park in the United States is around $300 per month.

When investing in mobile home parks, it's important to conduct thorough due diligence and research to ensure that the park meets your investment goals and criteria. This may include evaluating the park's location, occupancy rates, rental fees, and potential for growth. By taking the time to carefully research potential mobile home park investments, investors can make informed investment decisions and generate passive income over the long term.

Self-Storage Units

Self-storage units can be a lucrative investment opportunity for those looking to generate passive income. As the demand for affordable storage space continues to grow, the self-storage industry has seen a steady increase in profitability over the years. Investing in self-storage units allows individuals to earn a steady stream of income without the hassle of managing traditional rental properties. Here are some ways that they can generate passive income:

1. *Rental income*: Self-storage units generate rental income from tenants who lease the space to store their belongings. This is typically the primary source of income for self-storage facilities.
2. *Late fees and other charges*: Self-storage facilities can also generate income from late fees, administrative fees, and other charges related to the rental of storage units.
3. *Ancillary services*: Some self-storage facilities may offer ancillary services such as truck rentals, moving supplies, or packing and unpacking services. These services can generate additional income for the facility.
4. *Property appreciation*: Like other types of real estate investments, self-storage facilities value may appreciate over time, providing investors with capital gains if they decide to sell the property.

To generate passive income from self-storage units, investors can purchase an existing facility or develop a new one. Investing in an existing facility may require less upfront capital but may also come with the risk of inheriting any existing problems or issues. Developing a new facility may require more upfront capital but offers the opportunity to build a facility that meets specific needs and can be designed for maximum efficiency and profitability.

There are several ways to find self-storage units for purchase:

1. *Real estate websites*: Many real estate websites, such as *LoopNet*, offer listings for self-storage facilities for sale.

2. *Auction websites*: Websites such as ***StorageAuctions.com*** and ***StorageTreasures.com*** list self-storage facilities that are up for auction.
3. *Real estate agents*: Contacting a commercial real estate agent who specializes in self-storage properties can help you find listings and assist you in the purchasing process.
4. *Networking*: Attend industry conferences, seminars, and events to network with other self-storage investors and operators who may know of facilities for sale.
5. *Online marketplaces*: Websites such as ***CREXi*** and ***Brevitas*** offer commercial real estate listings, including self-storage facilities for sale.

Self-Storage Units can be a unique source of passive income, but there are some things to be aware of before investing:

1. *Analyze the facility*: Look at the physical condition of the facility, including the condition of the units, security measures, and accessibility. Assess the potential for revenue growth by looking at the occupancy rates, rental rates, and revenue history of the facility.
2. *Understand the costs*: Consider the costs associated with owning and operating a self-storage facility, including maintenance and repair costs, property taxes, and insurance.
3. *Consider financing options*: Explore financing options for purchasing a self-storage facility, such as a commercial mortgage or Small Business Administration (SBA) loan.
4. *Hire a professional*: Consider hiring a professional, such as a real estate agent, attorney, or accountant, to assist you in the purchasing process and ensure you're making a wise investment.
5. *Develop a management plan*: Develop a plan for managing the facility, including marketing strategies, rental agreements, and customer service.

In general, rental rates for self-storage units can range from $50 to $200 per month, depending on the size of the unit, location, and amenities offered. The average monthly rental rate for a 10x10 storage unit in the United States is around $100.

Overall, investing in self-storage units for passive income rental can be a lucrative investment, but it's important to do your research and understand the costs and potential for revenue growth before making a purchase. As with any real estate investment, it's important to do your due diligence before investing in a self-storage facility.

Crowdfunding Real Estate

Crowdfunding real estate is a relatively new investment opportunity that allows individuals to invest in real estate projects with a small amount of money. Essentially, it is a way for investors to pool their funds together to invest in larger real estate projects.

There are two types of crowdfunding real estate: equity-based and debt-based. In equity-based crowdfunding, investors own a share of the property and receive a portion of the profits generated from the property. In debt-based crowdfunding, investors act as lenders and receive a fixed return on their investment in the form of interest payments.

To participate in crowdfunding real estate, investors can sign up on crowdfunding platforms such as *Fundrise*, *RealtyMogul*, or *PeerStreet*. These platforms vet and select real estate projects and offer investors the opportunity to invest in them. Investors can browse through different real estate projects, read project descriptions and financial statements, and decide which projects to invest in. Some platforms may have minimum investment requirements, while others may allow investors to invest as little as $100.

It is important for investors to conduct their due diligence and research the platform and real estate project, financials, and fees thoroughly before investing.

The potential return on investment for crowdfunding real estate can vary, but it typically ranges from 6% to 12%, depending on the specific investment opportunity and the performance of the real estate market. While crowdfunding real estate can provide passive income, it's also a relatively new and less tested investment model, which may come with higher risks.

Investing in crowdfunding real estate can provide passive income in the form of dividends, rental income, or interest payments, depending on the type of investment. It can also provide diversification to an investment portfolio and access to real estate investments that may have been previously unavailable to individual investors.

Chapter 2: Finance & Investment Opportunities

Dividend Stocks

Dividend stocks are stocks that pay out a portion of the company's profits to shareholders in the form of regular dividends. This can be a great way to generate passive income, as investors can earn a regular income stream without having to sell their shares.

Dividend stocks typically come from established companies with a track record of steady profits and growth. These companies may operate in a variety of industries, including consumer goods, healthcare, technology, and finance. To generate passive income from dividend stocks, investors can purchase shares of individual companies that offer a dividend or invest in dividend-focused exchange-traded funds (ETFs) or mutual funds.

It's important to note that the value of dividend stocks can fluctuate based on the performance of the underlying company and broader market conditions. However, dividend-paying stocks have historically provided higher returns and less volatility than non-dividend-paying stocks, making them a popular choice for income-focused investors.

Historically, some of the highest yielding dividend stocks have come from industries such as energy, utilities, and real estate investment trusts (REITs). However, it's important to note that high yields can also indicate higher risk and that a company's financial health and dividend growth history should be considered alongside yield when evaluating potential investments.

Investors can use stock screening tools and financial news sources to identify high-yielding dividend stocks. Some popular stock screening tools include *Yahoo Finance*, *Google Finance*, and *Seeking Alpha*, which allow investors to screen for stocks with specific yield and financial criteria. Additionally, financial news sources such as *CNBC* and *Bloomberg* often provide updates on the highest yielding dividend stocks in current market conditions.

When selecting dividend stocks or funds, it's important to consider factors such as the company's financial health, dividend history and growth, and the overall diversification of the portfolio. Investors should also keep in mind that dividend income is subject to taxation, so it's important to consult with a financial advisor to understand the tax implications of investing in dividend stocks.

According to historical data, the average dividend yield for stocks in the S&P 500 index is around 1.9%. This means that if you invested $100,000 in a diversified portfolio of dividend stocks with an average yield of 1.9%, you could expect to earn around $1,900 in annual dividends. However, it's important to remember that the actual amount of passive income you earn will depend on the specific stocks you choose and the performance of the stock market.

It's important to note that investors should conduct their own due diligence and consult with a financial advisor before making any investment decisions.

Peer-to-Peer Lending

Peer-to-peer (P2P) lending is an alternative investment option that allows individuals to lend money directly to other individuals or small businesses through online platforms. P2P lending can generate passive income in the form of interest earned on the loans.

To start investing in P2P lending, investors first need to find a reputable P2P lending platform. Popular P2P lending platforms include *LendingClub*, *Prosper*, and *Upstart*. Once an investor has signed up for an account and completed any necessary KYC and AML requirements, they can start browsing available loans to invest in.

On P2P lending platforms, loans are typically graded by risk level, with higher-risk loans offering higher interest rates. Investors can choose to invest in individual loans or spread their investment across multiple loans to diversify their portfolio and minimize risk. Most P2P lending platforms also offer automated investment tools that allow investors to set criteria for loans they want to invest in and have their investments automatically allocated.

It's important to note that P2P lending carries some risk, as borrowers may default on their loans, leading to loss of principal for the investor. Investors should carefully evaluate the risk and return profile of each loan and diversify their investments across multiple loans to minimize risk.

Peer-to-peer (P2P) lending can be a source of passive income, but there are some things to be aware of before investing:

1. *Risk*: P2P lending involves lending money to individuals or businesses through an online platform. As with any lending, there is the risk of default, which can result in lost principal and interest. Make sure to understand the risks involved before investing.
2. *Platform fees*: P2P lending platforms typically charge fees for their services. Make sure to understand the fee structure before investing and factor them into your potential returns.
3. *Diversification*: To minimize risk, it's important to diversify your investments across a variety of borrowers and loans. This can help

spread the risk and reduce the impact of any individual loan default.

4. ***Underwriting process***: Make sure to research the underwriting process of the P2P lending platform to understand how borrowers are evaluated and selected. A strong underwriting process can help reduce the risk of default.

5. ***Liquidity***: P2P loans typically have a fixed term, which means that your investment is tied up for a certain period. Make sure to understand the liquidity terms of the platform before investing.

6. ***Regulation***: P2P lending is subject to regulation, and different countries and regions may have different rules and requirements. Make sure to research the regulatory environment and any potential risks or limitations before investing.

7. ***Tax implications***: P2P lending income may be subject to taxation. Make sure to understand the tax implications of your investment and consult with a tax professional if necessary.

According to some estimates, P2P lending investors can expect to earn annual returns ranging from 5% to 10%. However, there are risks involved with P2P lending, such as borrower default, and past performance is not a guarantee of future returns.

P2P lending can be a good option for investors looking to generate passive income with relatively low minimum investments and potentially higher yields than traditional fixed-income investments. However, investors should carefully evaluate the risks and consult with a financial advisor before making any investment decisions.

Mutual Funds

Mutual funds are investment vehicles that pool money from many investors to purchase a diversified portfolio of stocks, bonds, or other securities. Mutual funds can generate passive income in several ways.

First, mutual funds can generate income through dividend payments from the stocks held in the fund. When a company pays a dividend to its shareholders, the mutual fund receives a portion of that payment based on the number of shares it holds in the company. The mutual fund then passes on this income to its investors in the form of distributions.

Second, mutual funds can generate income through interest payments from the bonds held in the fund. When a bond pays interest, the mutual fund receives a portion of that payment based on the amount of the bond it holds. The mutual fund then passes on this income to its investors in the form of distributions.

Third, some mutual funds are designed to generate income by investing in securities that pay higher yields, such as high-dividend stocks or high-yield bonds. These funds may generate higher income than traditional mutual funds, but they may also carry higher risk.

It's important to note that mutual funds also carry some risk, as the value of the fund's holdings can fluctuate based on market conditions. Additionally, mutual funds charge fees, which can eat into the income generated by the fund.

When looking for the best yielding mutual funds, there are several factors to consider:

1. *Yield*: The yield of a mutual fund represents the income generated by the fund's holdings. Look for mutual funds with a high yield but be sure to compare the yield to the fund's risk and return profile.
2. *Expense ratio*: The expense ratio represents the fees charged by the mutual fund company to manage the fund. Look for mutual funds with a low expense ratio to maximize your investment return.

3. *Historical performance*: Look at the fund's historical performance over the long term to determine how well it has performed. Keep in mind that past performance does not guarantee future results.
4. *Risk level*: Mutual funds carry varying levels of risk based on their investment strategy and holdings. Be sure to evaluate the fund's risk level and compare it to your personal risk tolerance.
5. *Fund manager experience*: Look at the experience and track record of the fund manager to determine their ability to generate strong returns over time.

To find the best yielding mutual funds, you can use various online tools and resources such as *Morningstar, Yahoo Finance*, and *Google Finance*. These resources provide information on a mutual fund's yield, expense ratio, historical performance, risk level, and fund manager experience.

According to historical data, the average annual return for mutual funds has been around 8-10%, although returns can vary widely depending on the performance of the fund and the market conditions. It's important to keep in mind that past performance is not a guarantee of future returns, and there are risks involved with investing in mutual funds, such as market volatility and fund management fees.

Overall, mutual funds can be a good option for investors looking to generate passive income through diversified investments in stocks, bonds, or other securities. Investors should carefully evaluate the risk and return profile of each fund and consult with a financial advisor before making any investment decisions.

ETFs (Exchange Traded Funds)

Exchange Traded Funds (ETFs) are investment funds that are traded on stock exchanges like individual stocks. ETFs can generate passive income in several ways.

First, ETFs can generate income through dividend payments from the stocks held in the fund. When a company pays a dividend to its shareholders, the ETF receives a portion of that payment based on the number of shares it holds in the company. The ETF then passes on this income to its investors in the form of distributions.

Second, ETFs can generate income through interest payments from the bonds held in the fund. When a bond pays interest, the ETF receives a portion of that payment based on the amount of the bond it holds. The ETF then passes on this income to its investors in the form of distributions.

Third, some ETFs are designed to generate income by investing in securities that pay higher yields, such as high-dividend stocks or high-yield bonds. These ETFs may generate higher income than traditional ETFs, but they may also carry higher risk.

It's important to note that ETFs also carry some risk, as the value of the fund's holdings can fluctuate based on market conditions. Additionally, ETFs charge fees, which can eat into the income generated by the fund.

When looking for the best yielding ETFs, there are several factors to consider:

1. *Yield*: The yield of an ETF represents the income generated by the ETF's holdings. Look for ETFs with a high yield but be sure to compare the yield to the ETF's risk and return profile.
2. *Expense ratio*: The expense ratio represents the fees charged by the ETF company to manage the fund. Look for ETFs with a low expense ratio to maximize your investment return.
3. *Historical performance*: Look at the ETF's historical performance over the long term to determine how well it has performed. Keep in mind that past performance does not guarantee future results.

4. ***Risk level***: ETFs carry varying levels of risk based on their investment strategy and holdings. Be sure to evaluate the ETF's risk level and compare it to your personal risk tolerance.

5. ***Index tracking***: ETFs are designed to track a specific index, such as the S&P 500 or Dow Jones Industrial Average. Look for ETFs that track well-performing and diversified indexes.

To find the best yielding ETFs, you can use various online tools and resources such as **Morningstar**, *Yahoo Finance*, and *Google Finance*. These resources provide information on an ETF's yield, expense ratio, historical performance, risk level, and index tracking. You can also consult with a financial advisor who can help you identify and evaluate ETFs that meet your investment goals and risk tolerance. Additionally, you can explore ETFs that focus on high-yield investments such as dividend-paying stocks or high-yield bonds.

According to historical data, the average annual return for ETFs has been around 8-10%, although returns can vary widely depending on the performance of the ETF and the market conditions. It's important to keep in mind that past performance is not a guarantee of future returns, and there are risks involved with investing in ETFs, such as market volatility and ETF management fees.

Overall, ETFs can be a good option for investors looking to generate passive income through diversified investments in stocks, bonds, or other securities. Investors should carefully evaluate the risk and return profile of each ETF and consult with a financial advisor before making any investment decisions.

Royalties

Royalties are a form of passive income that can be earned by owning the rights to intellectual property, such as music, books, patents, and trademarks. The owner of the intellectual property earns a percentage of the revenue generated by its use or licensing.

There are several ways to earn royalties and generate passive income:

1. *Music royalties*: If you own the rights to a song or musical composition, you can earn royalties when it is played on the radio, streaming services, or other media. You can also earn royalties when your music is licensed for use in television shows, movies, commercials, and other media.
2. *Book royalties*: If you are an author or publisher, you can earn royalties on book sales. The percentage of royalties earned varies based on the contract with the publisher.
3. *Patent royalties*: If you have a patent for an invention, you can earn royalties when it is licensed for use by another company.
4. *Trademark royalties*: If you own a trademark, you can earn royalties when it is licensed for use by other companies.

To earn royalties, you must first own the intellectual property rights. You can acquire these rights by creating original works or purchasing the rights from others. Once you own the rights, you can license them to other companies or individuals for use. The terms of the license agreement will specify the percentage of revenue you will earn as royalties.

To purchase music rights from others, you can consider contacting music publishers or searching online music marketplaces. Here are a few options to explore:

1. *Music publishers*: You can contact music publishers directly to inquire about purchasing music rights. Some popular music publishers include *Sony/ATV*, *Universal Music Publishing Group*, and *Warner/Chappell Music*.
2. *Royalty exchange websites*: Websites like *Royalty Exchange* allow you to purchase existing music royalties. You can bid on the

royalties of a particular song or artist and potentially earn passive income from the future earnings generated by those royalties.

There are several companies that specialize in managing and licensing intellectual property rights, such as BMI, ASCAP, and SESAC for music royalties, and the United States Patent and Trademark Office for patent royalties. These companies can help you manage and monetize your intellectual property to generate passive income. Additionally, you can work with a lawyer or intellectual property specialist to help you navigate the legal aspects of royalty agreements and ensure that you are getting a fair share of the revenue generated by your intellectual property.

The average music royalty rate can vary widely depending on several factors, such as the type of music royalty (mechanical or performance), the country or region where the music is being played, and the specific terms of the agreement between the songwriter or publisher and the entity using the music.

For mechanical royalties, the rate is typically set by law and can vary by country. In the United States, the mechanical royalty rate for physical recordings is currently 9.1 cents per song per unit, while the rate for digital downloads and streaming is 9.1 cents per song or 1.75 cents per minute of playing time, whichever is greater.

For performance royalties, the rate can vary depending on the type of performance and the entity using the music. For example, in the United States, the rate for public performances of music on the radio is set by the Copyright Royalty Board and currently ranges from $0.0014 to $0.0025 per performance per listener, depending on the size of the station and the type of music being played. The rate for public performances of music in a venue such as a concert hall or nightclub is typically negotiated between the songwriter or publisher and the venue owner or promoter.

The amount of passive income you can earn from book royalties varies widely depending on factors such as the genre of the book, the publisher, the distribution channels, and the marketing efforts.

For traditional publishing, the standard royalty rate for authors is typically between 8% and 15% of the book's net sales. However, some publishers may offer higher royalty rates for established authors or for certain genres.

For self-publishing, the royalty rates can be higher, usually ranging from 35% to 70% of the book's sale price, depending on the platform and distribution channels used.

Patent royalties are usually paid as a percentage of the sales revenue generated from the patented product or technology. The typical royalty rate for patents ranges from 1% to 10% of the sales price, although it can be higher or lower depending on the factors mentioned above.

Trademark royalties are usually paid as a percentage of the revenue generated by the licensee from using the trademark. The typical royalty rate for trademarks ranges from 5% to 10% of the licensee's gross sales, although it can be higher or lower depending on the factors mentioned above.

Before making any purchases, it's important to do your research and ensure that you understand the terms and conditions of the music rights you are purchasing.

Annuities

Annuities can be a way to generate passive income in retirement. An annuity is a financial product that is typically offered by insurance companies, and it is designed to provide a guaranteed stream of income for a set period or for the rest of your life.

When you purchase an annuity, you make a lump sum payment to the insurance company, and in return, the company promises to pay you a regular income stream over a specified period. There are several different types of annuities available, but the two most common types are immediate annuities and deferred annuities.

With an immediate annuity, you make a lump sum payment to the insurance company, and the company begins paying you a guaranteed income stream right away. The amount of the income stream is determined by several factors, including your age, the size of your initial investment, and the type of annuity you choose.

With a deferred annuity, you make a lump sum payment to the insurance company, but the payments do not start immediately. Instead, the money is invested and grows tax-deferred until you decide to start receiving payments. This can be a good option if you are still working and want to save for retirement. Here are some steps you can take to find the right annuity for you:

1. *Understand your financial goals*: Before purchasing an annuity, it's important to understand your financial goals and how an annuity can help you achieve them. Are you looking for guaranteed income for life, or are you trying to build wealth for retirement?
2. *Determine your risk tolerance*: Annuities come in different types with varying levels of risk. You should determine your risk tolerance before selecting an annuity. If you're risk-averse, a fixed annuity may be a better option for you. If you're comfortable with market fluctuations, a variable annuity may be a good fit.
3. *Consider the type of annuity*: There are several types of annuities, including fixed, variable, indexed, and immediate annuities. Each

has its own features and benefits, so it's important to understand the differences and choose the right type for you.

4. ***Shop around***: Annuities are offered by insurance companies, so it's important to shop around and compare offerings from different insurers. Look at the fees, surrender charges, and interest rates associated with each annuity.

5. ***Consult with a financial advisor***: An annuity is a complex financial product, so it's important to consult with a financial advisor before deciding. An advisor can help you determine if an annuity is right for you and which type would be the best fit for your financial goals and risk tolerance.

Typically, annuities pay out a fixed income for a set period, such as ten or twenty years, or for the rest of your life. The amount of income you receive each month or year is determined by the size of your investment, the interest rate, and the annuity's payment structure.

For example, if you invest $100,000 in an annuity that pays a fixed rate of 5% per year and guarantees a payout for the rest of your life, you could expect to receive $5,000 per year in passive income. The exact amount you receive will depend on the specific terms of your annuity.

Annuities can be a good option for generating passive income because they provide a guaranteed income stream for a set period or for the rest of your life. However, it's important to note that annuities can be expensive, and they may not be the best option for everyone. Before investing in an annuity, it's important to do your research and consult with a financial advisor to determine if it's the right choice for you.

Private Equity Investing

Private equity investing involves investing in privately held companies that are not traded on public exchanges. This type of investment can generate passive income in a few different ways.

Firstly, private equity investors can receive dividends from the companies they invest in. This is like receiving dividends from a stock investment, but with private equity, the dividends may be less frequent and less predictable.

Secondly, private equity investors can generate passive income through capital appreciation. When the company grows in value, the value of the investor's shares increases as well. This can lead to significant returns if the company is successful.

Finally, private equity investors can generate passive income through selling their shares in the company. This can happen through an initial public offering (IPO), where the company goes public and the investor can sell their shares on the stock market, or through a sale to another company or investor.

Private equity investing typically requires a higher minimum investment and may be less liquid than other types of investments, but it can also offer the potential for higher returns. It is important to thoroughly research and understand the risks associated with private equity investments before investing. Private equity investments are typically only available to accredited investors, who meet certain income and net worth requirements. Here are some ways to find private equity investment opportunities:

1. *Use online platforms*: There are online platforms such as *AngelList, SeedInvest*, and *Fundable* that connect investors with private equity investment opportunities.
2. *Join an investment club or network*: Joining an investment club or network can provide access to private equity investment opportunities. These clubs or networks can be found online or in

person and are typically comprised of individuals who are interested in investing in private equity.

3. ***Contact private equity firms***: Private equity firms can be found through online directories or industry associations. Contacting these firms directly can provide information about their investment opportunities.

4. ***Attend industry conferences***: Attending industry conferences can provide opportunities to network with private equity professionals and learn about investment opportunities.

In general, private equity investments are considered high risk but can also provide high returns, with some estimates suggesting an average return of around 10-15% per year. However, the actual returns can vary widely and may be lower or higher depending on the specific investment.

It's important to note that private equity investments carry significant risks and should be thoroughly researched before investing. It's recommended that individuals consult with a financial advisor or professional before making any investment decisions.

Angel Investing

Angel investing is a method of investing in early-stage businesses and startups that have high growth potential. It involves providing financial support to entrepreneurs in exchange for ownership equity or convertible debt.

Angel investing can generate passive income in two ways: capital appreciation and dividends. When a startup grows in value and becomes more profitable, the value of an angel investor's ownership stake also increases, resulting in capital appreciation. Additionally, some startups may choose to issue dividends to their investors in order to distribute profits.

To get started with angel investing, individuals should first have a thorough understanding of the process and the risks involved. It is important to conduct due diligence on potential startups, including analyzing their business plan, financials, and leadership team. It can also be helpful to network with other angel investors and attend industry events to learn about new investment opportunities.

Angel investors can find investment opportunities through various channels, including online platforms, investment networks, and referrals from other investors or entrepreneurs. Online platforms, such as *AngelList* and *SeedInvest*, allow accredited investors to browse and invest in startups online. Investment networks, such as the **Angel Capital Association** and the **National Venture Capital Association**, provide resources and connections for angel investors. Referrals from other investors or entrepreneurs can also be a valuable source of investment opportunities.

The amount of money one expects to make through angel investing for passive income can vary widely and depends on various factors such as the success of the companies invested in, the type of angel investment made, and the length of the investment period. In general, angel investments are considered high risk but can also provide high returns, with some estimates suggesting an average return of around 25-30% per year. However, the actual returns can vary widely and may be lower or higher depending on the specific investment.

It is important to note that angel investing involves significant risk, as many startups fail to become profitable. Investors should carefully evaluate the potential risks and rewards of each investment opportunity and be prepared to lose their entire investment. It is recommended that individuals consult with a financial advisor before making any angel investments.

Options Trading

Options trading is a type of investing strategy that involves buying and selling options contracts. An options contract is a financial derivative that gives the holder the right, but not the obligation, to buy or sell an underlying asset at a predetermined price within a specific timeframe. The two main types of options contracts are call options and put options.

To generate passive income through options trading, an investor can sell options contracts, also known as writing options. When an investor writes a call option, they receive a premium, or payment, from the buyer of the option in exchange for agreeing to sell the underlying asset at a certain price if the buyer chooses to exercise the option. Similarly, when an investor writes a put option, they receive a premium from the buyer of the option in exchange for agreeing to buy the underlying asset at a certain price if the buyer chooses to exercise the option.

The key to successful options trading for passive income is to carefully manage risk. Selling options contracts can generate consistent income, but it also exposes the seller to potential losses if the underlying asset moves in an unexpected direction. As such, it is important to have a solid understanding of options trading and to employ sound risk management strategies such as setting stop-loss orders and avoiding over-leveraging.

To get started with options trading for passive income, investors can open an options trading account with a reputable online broker, such as **E*TRADE** or **TD Ameritrade**, and start practicing with a virtual trading account. It is also recommended to read books and articles, watch educational videos, and take courses on options trading to gain a deeper understanding of the mechanics and risks involved.

Options trading can be risky and complex, and it's important to understand the potential dangers before investing. Here are some of the main risks to be aware of:

1. *Limited lifespan*: Options contracts have a limited lifespan and expire on a specific date. This means that if the trade doesn't go in

your favor before the expiration date, you could lose your entire investment.

2. *Volatility*: Options prices can be highly volatile and can change quickly, which can lead to significant losses if you're not careful.

3. *Leverage*: Options trading allows investors to control a large amount of stock for a relatively small amount of money. While this can lead to big gains, it can also amplify losses.

4. *Complexity*: Options trading can be complex, with a variety of different strategies and variables to consider. This can make it challenging for novice investors to navigate.

5. *Lack of liquidity*: Options markets can be illiquid at times, which means it can be difficult to buy or sell options at a fair price.

Overall, options trading can be a powerful tool for generating passive income, but it's important to approach it with caution and make sure you fully understand the risks involved.

Earn Interest from High-Yield Savings Accounts or CDs

Earning interest from high-yield savings accounts or CDs is one of the safest ways to generate passive income. A high-yield savings account is a type of savings account that offers a higher interest rate than a regular savings account. Similarly, a certificate of deposit (CD) is a savings account that pays a fixed interest rate over a set period.

To start earning passive income from high-yield savings accounts or CDs, you will first need to research and compare different financial institutions to find the ones that offer the highest interest rates. You can use online comparison tools or consult with a financial advisor to find the best options.

Once you have identified the institutions that offer the highest interest rates, you can open a high-yield savings account or CD and deposit your funds. Depending on the institution and the terms of the account or CD, you may be required to maintain a minimum balance or keep your funds locked in for a certain period to earn the maximum interest rate.

It's important to note that while high-yield savings accounts and CDs are safe and reliable sources of passive income, they often offer lower returns compared to other forms of investments such as stocks or real estate.

High-yield savings accounts and CDs can be found at a variety of financial institutions, including banks, credit unions, and online banks. Here are some steps to help you find high-yield options:

1. *Research online banks*: Online banks often offer higher interest rates on savings accounts and CDs than traditional brick-and-mortar banks. Look for online banks that are FDIC-insured and have a good reputation.
2. *Check credit unions*: Credit unions are member-owned financial institutions that often offer competitive rates on savings accounts and CDs. You may need to become a member to open an account, but many credit unions have relaxed eligibility requirements.

3. ***Compare rates***: Use online comparison tools or check directly with multiple banks and credit unions to compare interest rates on savings accounts and CDs. Look for accounts with the highest rates and make sure to check for any fees or restrictions.
4. ***Consider the term***: CDs have fixed terms, ranging from a few months to several years. Generally, the longer the term, the higher the interest rate. Decide how long you can afford to leave your money in the account and choose a term that fits your needs.
5. ***Understand the risks***: CDs and savings accounts are considered low-risk investments, but there is still the risk of inflation reducing the value of your savings over time. Make sure to consider the potential returns and risks before investing.

Currently, the average interest rate for a high yield savings account is around 0.5% to 1.5%, while the average interest rate for a 1-year CD is around 0.5% to 1.5%.

Remember to always do your research and understand the terms and conditions of any account before opening it.

Investing in Cryptocurrency

Investing in cryptocurrency can be a lucrative way to generate passive income. Cryptocurrencies like Bitcoin, Ethereum, and Litecoin have gained popularity over the years, and their value has increased significantly, leading to substantial profits for investors. The concept of cryptocurrency is based on blockchain technology, a decentralized and transparent system that allows secure transactions without the need for a central authority. This has made cryptocurrencies an attractive investment option for people around the world.

To generate passive income through cryptocurrency, one can invest in a cryptocurrency that has potential for growth and hold onto it for an extended period. Cryptocurrencies are known for their volatility, and their value can fluctuate significantly in a short period. However, investing in a promising cryptocurrency with a long-term strategy can help mitigate the risk of volatility and increase the chances of generating passive income.

Another way to generate passive income through cryptocurrency is by staking. Staking is a process where investors hold their cryptocurrency in a wallet and receive rewards for securing the network. This requires a certain amount of cryptocurrency to be locked up for a particular period, but the rewards can provide a steady stream of passive income.

Investing in cryptocurrency can also involve trading. Trading involves buying and selling cryptocurrencies to take advantage of price fluctuations in the market. While this method requires more active involvement and knowledge of the market, it can generate substantial profits if done correctly.

It is important to note that investing in cryptocurrency does come with its risks, and it is essential to do thorough research before investing. Cryptocurrencies are unregulated and subject to sudden changes, making it important to diversify one's portfolio and invest only what they can afford to lose.

There are a variety of resources available for investing in cryptocurrency. Here are some options:

1. *Cryptocurrency Exchanges*: These are online platforms where you can buy, sell, and trade cryptocurrencies. Some popular exchanges include *Coinbase*, *Binance*, *Kraken*, and *Gemini*.
2. *Cryptocurrency Wallets*: These are digital wallets that allow you to store your cryptocurrencies securely. Some popular wallets include *Trezor*, *Ledger*, and *Exodus*.
3. *Cryptocurrency Forums*: These are online communities where cryptocurrency enthusiasts can discuss trends, news, and investment strategies. Some popular forums include *Bitcointalk*, *Reddit's r/cryptocurrency*, and *CryptoCompare*.
4. *News Websites*: Keeping up with the latest news and trends in the cryptocurrency world can be crucial for making informed investment decisions. Some popular news websites include *CoinDesk*, *CryptoSlate*, and *Cointelegraph*.
5. *Cryptocurrency Courses*: For those who are new to cryptocurrency investing, taking a course can be a great way to learn the basics and get started on the right foot. Some popular courses include those offered by *Udemy*, *Coursera*, and *Coin Academy*.
6. *Social Media*: Social media platforms like *Twitter* and *Telegram* can be great sources of information for cryptocurrency investors. Following industry influencers and thought leaders can provide valuable insights and analysis.
7. *Cryptocurrency Research Reports*: Many financial firms and investment companies produce research reports on cryptocurrency and blockchain technology. These reports can provide in-depth analysis of market trends and investment opportunities.

Investing in cryptocurrency can be a source of passive income, but there are some things to be aware of before investing:

1. *Volatility*: Cryptocurrency prices can be highly volatile, which means that your investment can fluctuate significantly in value over short periods of time. Make sure to understand the risks involved and consider investing only what you can afford to lose.
2. *Regulation*: Cryptocurrency is a relatively new asset class, and regulations are still evolving in many countries and regions. Make

sure to understand the regulatory environment in your jurisdiction and any potential risks or limitations before investing.

3. *Security*: Cryptocurrency exchanges and wallets can be vulnerable to hacking and theft. Make sure to use a reputable exchange and implement strong security measures to protect your investments.

4. *Liquidity*: Cryptocurrency can be illiquid, which means that it may be difficult to buy or sell your investment quickly. Make sure to understand the liquidity of your investment and factor this into your investment strategy.

5. *Tax implications*: Cryptocurrency investment income may be subject to taxation. Make sure to understand the tax implications of your investment and consult with a tax professional if necessary.

6. *Investment strategy*: Cryptocurrency investing requires a solid investment strategy to maximize returns and minimize risk. Make sure to do your research and develop a strategy that aligns with your investment goals and risk tolerance.

The potential income from investing in cryptocurrency can vary widely depending on factors such as the type of cryptocurrency, market conditions, and individual investment strategies. Some investors have made significant profits from investing in cryptocurrencies, while others have experienced significant losses.

Investing in cryptocurrency carries significant risks, and it's important to do your research and invest responsibly. Always consult with a financial advisor before making any investment decisions.

Chapter 3: Digital Products

eBooks

With the rise of digital technology, eBooks have become a popular and convenient way for readers to access a vast array of literary content. However, eBooks also present a unique opportunity for writers and entrepreneurs to generate passive income. Unlike traditional publishing methods, self-publishing an eBook requires little to no upfront costs and can provide a steady stream of income for years to come.

eBooks can be a lucrative source of passive income for authors or publishers. Here's how:

1. *Write or create an eBook*: The first step to generating passive income through eBooks is to create one. You can write the eBook yourself or outsource the work to a freelance writer.
2. *Edit and format the eBook*: Once you have written the eBook, you need to edit and format it properly. Ensure that it is error-free, has a clear structure, and is visually appealing.
3. *Choose a platform to publish the eBook*: There are several platforms you can use to publish and sell your eBook, such as *Amazon's Kindle Direct Publishing*, *Barnes & Noble's Nook Press*, and *Apple's iBooks*. Choose a platform that suits your needs and budget.
4. *Set a price for the eBook*: Determine the price of your eBook based on factors such as the length, content, and niche of the eBook, as well as the competition.
5. *Market the eBook*: You need to promote your eBook to attract readers and generate sales. You can use various marketing techniques such as social media, email marketing, guest posting, and paid advertising.
6. *Collect the royalties*: Once your eBook is published and selling, you can sit back and collect the royalties. The amount of passive income you earn from eBooks will depend on the sales volume and price of your eBook, as well as the royalty rate offered by the platform.

There are many free resources available online to help you create an eBook, some of which are:

1. *Google Docs*: Google Docs is a free online word processing software that allows you to create and edit documents. You can use Google Docs to write your eBook and export it as a PDF.
2. *Canva*: Canva is a free graphic design platform that offers a range of templates for eBook covers and interior pages. You can also use Canva to create images and graphics to include in your eBook.
3. *Calibre*: Calibre is a free eBook management tool that allows you to convert your eBook into various formats, including EPUB, MOBI, and PDF.
4. *Sigil*: Sigil is a free open-source eBook editor that allows you to create and edit eBooks in EPUB format.
5. *Reedsy*: Reedsy is a free online platform that offers a range of tools to help you create and publish your eBook. It includes a book editor, formatting tools, and cover design templates.
6. *Leanpub*: Leanpub is a free eBook publishing platform that allows you to create and sell eBooks in various formats, including EPUB, MOBI, and PDF.
7. *Pressbooks*: Pressbooks is a free online publishing platform that allows you to create and publish eBooks in various formats. It includes a range of templates and formatting tools to help you create professional-looking eBooks.
8. *ChatGPT*: ChatGPT is a large language model developed by OpenAI, designed to respond to a wide range of prompts with human-like language understanding. It is a valuable resource to help you for idea prompts or to rework a sentence.
9. *Other AI*: Some alternatives to *ChatGPT* include *GPT-3, BERT, RoBERTa*, and *T5*, which are also large language models developed by various research organizations.

Investing in eBooks can be a source of passive income, but there are some things to be aware of before investing:

1. ***Market demand***: eBooks are a highly competitive market, and it's important to research the market demand for the type of content you are planning to invest in. Consider investing in a niche that has high demand and low competition.
2. ***Quality of content***: The quality of the content is critical for the success of an eBook. Make sure to invest in high-quality content that is well-written and provides value to the reader.
3. ***Marketing and promotion***: Investing in an eBook is not enough, it's also important to invest in marketing and promotion to get your eBook in front of your target audience. Consider investing in marketing strategies such as social media marketing, email marketing, and paid advertising.
4. ***Intellectual property***: Make sure to invest in eBooks that do not infringe on anyone's intellectual property rights. This can include trademarks, copyrights, and patents.
5. ***Royalty rates***: The royalty rates offered by publishing platforms can vary, and it's important to research and compare the rates offered by different platforms. Consider investing in a platform that offers a high royalty rate and provides transparency in their payment process.

The amount of passive income you can make with eBooks varies greatly depending on factors such as the quality of your content, your marketing strategy, and the price point of your book, but it is possible to earn anywhere from a few hundred to several thousand dollars per month.

Remember, while eBook publishing can be a great source of passive income, it requires hard work, dedication, and perseverance. You may not see immediate results, but with consistent effort, you can build a stream of passive income from eBooks.

Online Courses

Online courses can be a lucrative source of passive income. With the growing popularity of online learning, there is a huge demand for high-quality courses that provide valuable information to learners. To create an online course, you can follow these steps:

1. *Choose a topic*: Identify a topic that you are passionate about and have expertise in. Research the demand for your topic and see if there is a market for it.
2. *Plan your course*: Create a course outline, lesson plan, and decide on the teaching style you will use. Consider the duration of the course and the type of learners you are targeting.
3. *Create your course content*: Use various tools such as videos, audio recordings, and written materials to create your course content. Ensure your content is high-quality, engaging, and relevant to your learners.
4. *Choose a platform*: You can choose from several online course platforms such as *Udemy*, *Teachable*, and *Skillshare* to host and sell your course.
5. *Promote your course*: Once you have created your course and hosted it on a platform, you need to promote it to reach your target audience. Use social media, email marketing, and other advertising methods to promote your course.
6. *Continuously update your course*: To maintain interest and relevance, update your course content regularly, and engage with your learners by responding to their feedback and questions.

I know what you are thinking, so here are some ideas to generate topics for online courses:

1. *Teach a skill*: Identify a skill that you are good at, such as graphic design or coding, and create a course to teach others how to do it.
2. *Share your expertise*: If you have expertise in a certain field, such as marketing or finance, create a course to share your knowledge with others.

3. *Create a how-to course*: Identify a topic that people struggle with, such as meal planning or budgeting, and create a course that provides step-by-step instructions on how to do it.
4. *Teach a language*: If you are fluent in a second language, create a course to teach others how to speak it.
5. *Create a course on personal development*: Create a course on topics such as time management, goal setting, or mindfulness.
6. *Teach a hobby*: If you have a hobby that you are passionate about, such as photography or cooking, create a course to teach others how to do it.
7. *Create a course on entrepreneurship*: Share your knowledge on topics such as starting a business, marketing, or scaling.
8. *Teach a fitness class*: Create an online fitness course that people can follow at home.
9. *Create a course on mental health*: Create a course on topics such as managing anxiety, coping with depression, or improving relationships.
10. *Teach a course on a specific industry*: Create a course that provides an overview of a specific industry, such as real estate or technology.

These resources can help you to edit and improve your online course before you publish it to ensure that it is of high quality and effective in helping your students learn:

1. *Grammarly* - This is a popular online grammar checking tool that can help you to check your course for grammar and spelling errors.
2. *Hemingway Editor* - This tool helps you to simplify your writing and make it more readable.
3. *ProWritingAid* - This is another online editing tool that can help you to improve your writing by checking for grammar and spelling errors.
4. *Google Docs* - This is a free online word processing tool that allows you to collaborate with others and share your work for feedback.
5. *YouTube* - There are many free tutorials available on YouTube that can teach you how to edit your online course.

6. ***Udemy Studio*** - This is a free platform provided by Udemy for instructors to edit and publish their courses.
7. ***Canva*** - This is a free online design tool that can help you to create visual content for your course.

The potential earnings from online courses can vary widely depending on various factors such as the topic, quality of content, marketing strategy, and pricing structure, but some successful online course creators have reported earning tens or even hundreds of thousands of dollars per month in passive income.

Audio Books

Audio books can generate passive income by allowing authors or publishers to reach a wider audience and offer their content in a convenient format for busy individuals who prefer to listen rather than read. Audio books are popular for long commutes, workouts, and household chores, making them a popular choice for many consumers.

To create an audio book, an author or publisher can record the book using their own equipment or hire a professional narrator and audio engineer. The audio book can then be distributed through various channels, such as *Audible*, *iTunes*, and *Amazon*, or through the author's own website.

Audio books can generate passive income through royalties paid by the distributor or through direct sales made by the author or publisher. The amount of royalties or revenue earned from audio books will depend on factors such as the pricing strategy, distribution channels, and marketing efforts.

Here are some free resources to help you create an audiobook:

1. *Audacity* - a free, open-source audio editing software that allows you to record, edit, and mix your audio files.
2. *LAME MP3 encoder* - a free software that converts your audio files into MP3 format, which is the most common format used for audiobooks.
3. *Librivox* - a volunteer-run website that provides free audiobooks in the public domain. You can use this resource to listen to examples of well-narrated audiobooks.
4. *ACX* (Audiobook Creation Exchange) - an online marketplace for audiobook production. You can use this platform to connect with narrators and producers who can help you create your audiobook.
5. *YouTube* - you can find many tutorials and how-to videos on creating audiobooks on YouTube.
6. *Podium Audio* - a platform that allows you to distribute and monetize your audiobooks on various platforms, including Audible, Amazon, and iTunes.

7. *Canva* - a free graphic design platform that you can use to create cover art for your audiobook.
8. *Amazon Kindle Direct Publishing* - a platform that allows you to self-publish your audiobooks on Audible and Amazon.

If creating your own audio book isn't your cup of tea, you can always serve as the voice actor for another's work. Here are several resources to become a voice actor for audiobooks:

1. *ACX*: ACX is an audiobook creation platform that connects authors, publishers, and narrators. It offers a wide range of audiobook production resources and allows you to audition for audiobook projects.
2. *Voices.com*: Voices.com is an online marketplace for voice actors that offers audiobook narration opportunities.
3. *Edge Studio*: Edge Studio is a voice over production company that offers audiobook training and production services.
4. *Voice123*: Voice123 is an online platform that connects voice actors with clients, including those in need of audiobook narrators.
5. *Gravy for the Brain*: Gravy for the Brain is an online voice acting school that offers courses on audiobook narration, as well as other areas of voiceover work.
6. *The Voice Realm*: The Voice Realm is a platform that connects voice actors with clients looking for audiobook narrators.

If you are interested in creating and selling audiobooks for passive income, here are some things to be aware of:

1. *Production quality*: High-quality production is essential for audiobooks. Ensure that you have good equipment and a sound-proof recording area.
2. *Voiceover talent*: Choose a voiceover artist with a clear and pleasant voice that can convey the tone and mood of your book.
3. *Copyright laws*: Make sure you have the necessary rights and permissions to produce and sell an audiobook based on the original work.

4. *Distribution platforms*: Explore different audiobook distribution platforms such as *Audible*, *ACX*, and *Findaway Voices* to see which ones are best for your audiobook.
5. *Marketing*: Promote your audiobook through social media, email lists, and advertising to reach your target audience.
6. *Royalties*: Understand the royalty structure and payment terms of the platform you choose to distribute your audiobook on.
7. *Sales data and analytics*: Use sales data and analytics to make informed decisions about marketing and pricing strategies for your audiobook.

The amount of passive income you can make with audiobooks can vary widely depending on factors such as the popularity of the book, the royalty rate offered by the audiobook platform, and your marketing efforts, among others. According to some estimates, audiobook narrators and producers can earn anywhere from $100 to $500 per finished hour of audio, while successful authors can earn thousands of dollars per month in royalties from audiobook sales.

Creating an audio book requires careful planning and consideration of various factors, such as the length of the book, the choice of narrator, and the recording and editing process. However, with the right approach, audio books can be a valuable source of passive income for authors and publishers. Remember, creating an audiobook requires a significant investment of time and effort, so be prepared to devote a substantial amount of resources to the process.

Software as a Service (SaaS)

Software as a Service (SaaS) is a business model that allows users to access and use software applications over the internet. SaaS can be a great way to generate passive income because it requires minimal ongoing maintenance once the software is developed and deployed. Here are some ways that SaaS can generate passive income:

1. *Subscription-based model*: SaaS companies can charge users a monthly or yearly subscription fee to access the software. As long as customers continue to pay their subscription fees, the SaaS company can continue to generate passive income.

2. *Freemium model*: SaaS companies can offer a basic version of their software for free, with limited features. Users who want more advanced features can upgrade to a paid version of the software. This model allows the SaaS company to generate passive income from users who choose to upgrade.

3. *Licensing model*: SaaS companies can license their software to other businesses, allowing them to use it for a fee. This model can generate passive income for the SaaS company without requiring them to provide ongoing support or maintenance.

4. *Referral program*: SaaS companies can offer a referral program, where existing users are rewarded for referring new customers to the software. This can help the SaaS company to generate passive income through word-of-mouth marketing.

Here are some free resources to help bring your SaaS idea to reality:

1. *Product Hunt*: This platform helps you validate your SaaS idea by connecting you with a community of entrepreneurs, investors, and users who can provide feedback and support.

2. *Google Cloud Platform*: This cloud computing platform offers a range of tools and services for building and scaling your SaaS application, including storage, databases, analytics, and machine learning.

3. **GitHub**: This platform provides a code hosting and collaboration platform for developers to share and work on code together. You can use it to manage and organize your SaaS application's code.
4. **Stripe**: This payment processing platform provides tools and APIs for integrating payment processing into your SaaS application, making it easy to accept payments from customers.
5. **Trello**: This project management tool allows you to organize your SaaS development tasks and collaborate with your team members.
6. **Canva**: This graphic design tool can help you create professional-looking designs for your SaaS website and marketing materials.
7. **HubSpot**: This all-in-one marketing, sales, and customer service platform provides tools for managing and growing your SaaS business.
8. **Mailchimp**: This email marketing platform can help you build and grow your email list, which is important for promoting your SaaS application and communicating with your customers.
9. **Google Analytics**: This web analytics tool allows you to track and analyze user behavior on your SaaS application, helping you optimize and improve user experience.
10. **LinkedIn Learning**: This platform offers courses and tutorials on a wide range of topics related to SaaS development and business, helping you improve your skills and knowledge.

If you're considering creating a Software as a Service (SaaS) product for passive income, here are some things to be aware of:

1. **Market research**: Research the market to identify problems or needs that your SaaS product can solve or fulfill.
2. **Development costs**: Developing a SaaS product can be expensive, so consider the cost of development before committing to the project.
3. **Scalability**: Your SaaS product should be scalable to handle large numbers of users and data.
4. **Security**: Ensure that your SaaS product has strong security measures in place to protect user data.
5. **Customer support**: Provide excellent customer support to keep users engaged and happy with your product.

6. *Pricing*: Determine the appropriate pricing strategy for your SaaS product based on the features, value, and competition.
7. *Marketing and sales*: Use marketing and sales strategies to reach your target audience and build a user base.
8. *Continuous improvement*: Continuously update and improve your SaaS product to keep up with the market and user needs.
9. *Recurring revenue model*: SaaS products are typically sold on a subscription basis, so plan for a recurring revenue model for ongoing passive income.

Software as a Service (SaaS) can be a lucrative business model, and the amount you can make depends on various factors such as the market demand, pricing strategy, and customer acquisition costs. Some successful SaaS businesses generate millions of dollars in annual recurring revenue, while others may earn less. It's difficult to provide a specific figure as it can vary greatly depending on the nature of the software and the target market.

To create a successful SaaS product that generates passive income, it is important to focus on developing a product that meets the needs of your target audience, and to continuously update and improve the software to keep it competitive. It is also important to have a solid marketing strategy in place to attract new customers and retain existing ones.

Mobile Apps

Mobile apps can generate passive income by allowing users to purchase or subscribe to premium features within the app, displaying advertisements, or offering in-app purchases. The revenue generated from these actions can provide a continuous stream of income for the app owner.

To start generating passive income from mobile apps, the app must first be developed and launched on a platform such as the Apple App Store or Google Play Store. It is important to conduct market research to identify a need or demand for the app and to ensure that it provides value to potential users. Once developed, the app can be monetized using various strategies such as freemium models, subscription models, or offering in-app purchases.

Freemium models offer a basic version of the app for free, but charge users for access to premium features or content. Subscription models charge users a recurring fee for access to exclusive content or features within the app. In-app purchases allow users to buy virtual items, such as game upgrades or additional content, within the app.

To create a successful mobile app, it is essential to have strong design and development skills or to hire professionals to help bring the app to life. There are various free resources available to help learn mobile app development, such as online courses, tutorials, and forums. Additionally, platforms like the *Apple App Store* and *Google Play Store* provide resources for developers to optimize their app store listing and increase visibility to potential users.

There are several free resources available for bringing a mobile app idea to life:

1. **Appy Pie**: This is an online platform that allows you to create mobile apps without any coding experience. It offers a drag-and-drop interface, making it easy to use.

2. **Sketch**: This is a design tool that can be used to create prototypes of mobile apps. It's free to use and has a large community of designers who can provide feedback and support.
3. **Figma**: This is another design tool that can be used to create prototypes of mobile apps. It's free to use and allows you to collaborate with others in real-time.
4. **GitHub**: This is a platform that allows you to host your code and collaborate with other developers. It's free to use and has a large community of developers who can provide support.
5. **Google Firebase**: This is a mobile development platform that offers a range of tools for building mobile apps. It's free to use and offers features such as authentication, storage, and analytics.

There are several freelance options available to bring your mobile app idea to life, such as:

1. *Upwork*: Upwork is a global freelance platform that connects businesses with independent professionals. You can find developers, designers, and other experts to help you build your mobile app.
2. *Freelancer*: Freelancer is a platform that allows businesses to post their project requirements and receive bids from freelancers. You can find skilled developers and designers who specialize in building mobile apps.
3. *Toptal*: Toptal is a network of top freelance software developers and designers. They offer a rigorous screening process to ensure that you only work with the best freelancers.
4. *Fiverr*: Fiverr is a marketplace where you can find freelancers to help you with various aspects of your mobile app development, such as design, coding, testing, and more.
5. *Guru*: Guru is another freelance platform that connects businesses with freelancers. You can find developers, designers, and other professionals who can help you build your mobile app.

The potential income from mobile apps varies widely depending on several factors, such as the app's purpose, target audience, monetization strategy, marketing efforts, and overall popularity. Some apps generate very little revenue, while others can earn millions of dollars per year.

According to a recent study by Sensor Tower, the average revenue per download for a mobile app on the App Store is $0.95, while the average revenue per download for an app on Google Play is $0.23. However, these figures are just averages, and many factors can cause individual apps to earn more or less than these amounts.

Additionally, there are many ways to monetize a mobile app, such as in-app purchases, subscriptions, advertising, sponsorships, and more. The most successful apps often utilize multiple monetization strategies to maximize their earnings.

It is important to thoroughly research and vet potential freelancers to ensure they have the necessary skills and experience to bring your mobile app idea to life. Mobile apps can generate passive income through various monetization strategies and can be a lucrative source of income for app owners who create apps that provide value to their users.

Membership Sites

Membership sites are online platforms that offer exclusive content or services to individuals who pay a subscription fee to access it. These sites can generate passive income in several ways.

First, a membership site can provide recurring revenue streams by charging members a monthly or annual fee to access the content or services offered. If the site continues to provide value, members are likely to continue their subscriptions, providing a reliable source of passive income.

Second, membership sites can offer upsell opportunities. For example, a site may offer a basic membership level that provides access to certain content or services but offer additional levels at higher price points that offer even more valuable content or services. This allows the site to generate additional passive income from members who are willing to pay for more exclusive access.

Third, membership sites can be structured to encourage referrals and viral growth. For example, offering incentives to members who refer new members can help attract new subscribers and grow the site's revenue.

There are a variety of free resources available to help you create a membership site, depending on your level of expertise and the features you want to include. Here are a few options to consider:

1. *WordPress*: WordPress is a popular content management system that can be used to create a membership site. It offers a variety of plugins that allow you to create membership levels, restrict content, and manage payments. You can find a number of free and premium WordPress themes designed specifically for membership sites.
2. *Memberful*: Memberful is a membership platform that allows you to easily create a membership site without any coding or design skills. It integrates with WordPress and other website builders and offers features such as member management, content protection,

and payment processing. You can start with a free plan that supports up to 50 members.

3. *Mighty Networks*: Mighty Networks is a platform that allows you to create a social network or community around your membership site. It offers features such as member profiles, discussion forums, and private messaging, as well as tools for content creation and monetization. You can start with a free plan that supports up to 50 members.

4. *Teachable*: Teachable is a platform designed for creating and selling online courses, but it also includes features for creating a membership site. It offers tools for content creation, member management, and payment processing. You can start with a free plan that allows you to create and host unlimited courses.

5. *YouTube*: If you want to create a membership site focused on video content, you can consider using YouTube. YouTube offers features such as private videos, live streaming, and community engagement. You can use third-party tools such as *Patreon* or *Buy Me a Coffee* to manage membership subscriptions and payments.

Membership sites can be a great way to generate passive income, but there are several things you should be aware of before starting one. Here are some considerations:

1. *Content*: You need to have a steady stream of valuable content to keep members engaged and paying their subscription fees. This can be time-consuming and may require a team to help create and manage.

2. *Technology*: You need to have a platform that can handle member registration, payments, and access to exclusive content. There are many membership site plugins and platforms available, but it's important to choose one that meets your needs and budget.

3. *Marketing*: You need to have a plan for promoting your membership site and attracting new members. This may involve social media, email marketing, paid advertising, and other strategies.

4. *Customer Support*: You need to have a system in place for handling member inquiries, technical issues, and other support requests. Providing excellent customer service is essential for retaining members and building a positive reputation.
5. *Pricing*: You need to determine a pricing strategy that is both profitable and competitive. You may want to offer different membership tiers with different levels of access and pricing.
6. *Competition*: You need to research your competition and ensure that your membership site offers something unique and valuable that sets it apart from other options in the market.
7. *Legal Requirements*: You need to comply with any legal requirements for running a membership site, such as privacy laws, consumer protection laws, and payment processing regulations.
8. *Membership Retention*: You need to ensure that you are offering enough value to keep members paying their subscription fees over the long term. This may involve regularly adding new content, offering exclusive discounts or promotions, and creating a community around your membership site.

Membership sites can be a lucrative source of passive income, but the potential earnings can vary widely depending on the niche, the pricing, and the size of the audience. Some membership sites charge a monthly fee, while others charge an annual fee or a one-time fee for lifetime access.

To give a rough estimate, a membership site with 1000 members paying $50 per month would generate $50,000 in monthly recurring revenue. However, it can take time and effort to build up a membership base, and there are ongoing costs associated with maintaining the site and creating content.

Ultimately, the potential earnings from a membership site depend on factors such as the value proposition, marketing strategy, and retention rates, among others. Be sure to research and compare different options to find the best fit for your needs and budget. Membership sites can be an excellent way to generate passive income if they provide value and continue to meet the needs of their members.

Stock Photos

Stock photos are a type of visual content that can be licensed and used by individuals and businesses for various purposes, such as websites, social media, marketing materials, and more. Photographers and artists can create stock photos and upload them to online marketplaces, such as Shutterstock, Adobe Stock, and iStock, where they can be purchased by buyers looking for high-quality images.

As a photographer or artist, creating and selling stock photos can generate passive income because once the photos are uploaded and approved, they can continue to sell repeatedly without any additional effort or time on your part. The income earned from stock photos is usually based on a percentage of the licensing fee paid by the buyer, with some marketplaces offering a higher percentage for exclusive content.

To maximize the earning potential of your stock photos, it is important to consider the needs and trends of the market and create images that are in high demand. It is also important to upload consistently and keep your portfolio fresh with new and diverse content.

There are several free resources available to edit photos, including:

1. *GIMP*: GIMP is a free and open-source image editor that offers a wide range of tools and features similar to *Adobe Photoshop*. It is available for Windows, Mac, and Linux.
2. *Pixlr*: Pixlr is a free online photo editor that allows you to edit photos directly in your web browser. It offers a range of tools and features similar to Adobe Photoshop.
3. *Canva*: Canva is a graphic design platform that offers a range of design tools, including photo editing. It has a free version as well as a paid version with more features.
4. *Fotor*: Fotor is a free online photo editor that offers basic editing tools as well as some advanced features such as beauty retouching and HDR enhancement.

5. *Paint.net*: Paint.net is a free image editing software for Windows that offers a range of basic editing tools as well as some advanced features such as layers and plugins.
6. *Photopea*: Photopea is a free online photo editor that offers a range of tools and features similar to Adobe Photoshop. It supports a wide range of file formats and is compatible with most web browsers.

There are several resources where you can purchase affordable camera equipment:

1. *Amazon*: Amazon is one of the most popular and trusted online retailers where you can purchase camera equipment at an affordable price. They offer a wide range of cameras, lenses, and accessories from various brands.
2. *B&H Photo Video*: B&H Photo Video is another popular online retailer that offers a wide range of camera equipment at affordable prices. They also have a physical store in New York City.
3. *Adorama*: Adorama is a popular online retailer that offers a wide range of camera equipment at competitive prices. They also have a physical store in New York City.
4. *KEH Camera*: KEH Camera is a popular online retailer that specializes in used camera equipment. They offer a wide range of used cameras, lenses, and accessories at affordable prices.
5. *Craigslist*: Craigslist is a popular online marketplace where you can find used camera equipment at affordable prices. However, you should be cautious when purchasing from individual sellers and make sure to inspect the equipment thoroughly before making a purchase.
6. *eBay*: eBay is the largest online marketplace where you can find used camera equipment at affordable prices. However, you should be cautious when purchasing from individual sellers and make sure to inspect the equipment thoroughly when receiving your shipment. If anything is wrong, immediately open a case with eBay customer service.

On average, most stock photo agencies offer a commission rate of around 20-50% of the sale price of your photos, although some may offer higher or lower rates. The sale price of your photos will also depend on factors such as the size and resolution of the image, the license type (e.g., royalty-free, or rights-managed), and the usage rights granted to the buyer.

In terms of earnings, some photographers report earning a few hundred dollars per month from their stock photo sales, while others earn thousands of dollars per month. However, it's important to note that stock photography is generally not a get-rich-quick scheme, and it can take time and effort to build up a sizable portfolio and establish a regular income stream from stock photo sales.

There are also other ways to monetize your stock photos, such as selling them directly to clients, creating print-on-demand products, or using them in your own creative projects. Overall, stock photos can be a lucrative and passive income stream for photographers and artists with a talent for creating high-quality and in-demand visual content.

Website Flipping

Website flipping refers to the process of buying an existing website, improving its content and design, and then selling it for a profit. This strategy can generate passive income as the website's content can continue to generate revenue even after the website has been sold.

To start website flipping, you can first search for websites for sale on online marketplaces such as *Flippa*, *Empire Flippers*, and *Website Broker*. Once you have found a website that interests you, analyze its traffic, revenue, and expenses to determine its potential value.

To improve the website, you can make changes such as updating the design, creating new content, optimizing the website's SEO, and increasing traffic through advertising and social media promotion. Once the website has been improved, you can then list it for sale on the same online marketplaces or other websites such as *Facebook Marketplace* and *Craigslist*.

There are various free resources available for flipping websites, some of which are:

1. *Flippa Blog*: Flippa is a popular marketplace for buying and selling websites. Their blog has a lot of helpful articles on website flipping, including tips for finding websites to buy and how to improve the value of your website.
2. *Empire Flippers Podcast*: Empire Flippers is another popular website marketplace, and they have a podcast that covers topics related to website flipping. The podcast includes interviews with successful website flippers, as well as tips and strategies for buying and selling websites.
3. *YouTube*: There are many YouTube channels dedicated to website flipping, such as Flipping Websites and Flip Websites. These channels offer tutorials, case studies, and other helpful information for beginners and experienced website flippers alike.
4. *Facebook Groups*: There are many Facebook groups dedicated to website flipping, such as *Website Flippers Anonymous* and

Website Investing. These groups offer a place to connect with other website flippers, ask questions, and learn from experienced flippers.

5. *Reddit*: The *r/Flipping subreddit* has a dedicated section for website flipping, where you can find tips and advice from other website flippers.

6. *Blogs*: There are many blogs dedicated to website flipping, such as *FlipWebsites.com* and *WebsiteBroker.com*. These blogs offer helpful tips and advice on how to buy and sell websites, as well as case studies of successful flips.

Some successful website flippers report earning anywhere from a few thousand dollars to tens of thousands of dollars per month in profits, although these are typically individuals or companies with significant experience and resources to invest in website acquisition and improvement.

To maximize profits, it's important to buy websites at a reasonable price, make necessary improvements, and sell them at a higher price than what was paid initially. This can be a lucrative strategy for generating passive income, if you are willing to invest time and effort into improving the website.

Ad Revenue from Blogs or Websites

Ad revenue from blogs and websites can be a lucrative way to generate passive income. Website owners can earn money by displaying advertisements on their websites or blogs. Advertisers pay website owners to display ads on their websites, and the website owner earns money every time a user clicks on one of the ads.

To get started with ad revenue, website owners can sign up for advertising programs such as *Google AdSense*, which is a popular ad network that allows website owners to display ads on their website and earn money when users click on them. Other ad networks include *Media.net*, *Infolinks*, and *AdThrive*.

To increase ad revenue, website owners can focus on creating high-quality content that attracts a large and engaged audience. They can also optimize their website for search engines and ensure that their website is user-friendly and easy to navigate.

In addition to display ads, website owners can also earn money through affiliate marketing, where they earn a commission for promoting products or services on their website. They can also offer sponsored content or sponsored posts, where advertisers pay them to write a blog post or article that promotes their products or services.

There are several free resources that can help you attract advertisers to your website or blog:

1. *Google AdSense*: Google AdSense is a popular advertising program that allows you to display ads on your website. Advertisers bid on ad space, and you earn a commission when someone clicks on an ad.
2. *Media.net*: Media.net is an advertising network that allows you to display contextual ads on your website. The network is powered by Yahoo! and Bing, and it offers high-quality ads that are relevant to your content.

3. *BuySellAds*: BuySellAds is a marketplace where advertisers can buy ad space directly from publishers. The platform offers a wide range of ad formats and targeting options, and it's free to join.
4. *AdThrive*: AdThrive is an ad management company that helps publishers monetize their websites with high-quality ads. The company offers a variety of ad formats and optimization tools, and it has a minimum traffic requirement of 100,000 pageviews per month.
5. *Sovrn*: Sovrn is an ad network that offers a range of ad formats and targeting options. The company offers a free ad management tool called Meridian, which allows you to manage multiple ad networks from one dashboard.
6. *PropellerAds*: PropellerAds is an ad network that offers a variety of ad formats, including push notifications, pop-unders, and native ads. The network is known for its high-quality traffic and advanced targeting options.
7. *AdSense Alternative*: AdSense Alternative is a website that offers a list of alternative ad networks and monetization methods. The website is updated regularly and offers detailed information on each network.

Generating ad revenue from your blog or website can be a great way to earn passive income, but there are several things you should be aware of before starting:

1. *Traffic*: You need a significant amount of traffic to your website to generate significant ad revenue. This means focusing on SEO, social media marketing, and other strategies to increase your website's visibility.
2. *Ad Placement*: The placement of your ads is critical for maximizing revenue. You need to experiment with different ad placements and sizes to find what works best for your website and audience.
3. *Ad Quality*: The quality of your ads can impact user experience and revenue. Make sure the ads are relevant to your content and audience and avoid using too many ads or intrusive ad formats.

4. *Ad Networks*: There are many ad networks available, and you need to choose one that is reliable and offers competitive rates. Google AdSense is the most popular ad network, but there are other options available.
5. *Ad Blockers*: Many users use ad blockers, which can impact your revenue. You may want to consider using anti-ad blocker tools or strategies to encourage users to whitelist your site.
6. *Niche and Audience*: The niche and audience of your website can impact ad revenue. Some niches and demographics have higher advertising rates than others.
7. *Content Quality*: The quality of your content is critical for driving traffic and engagement. Make sure your content is informative, engaging, and high-quality to attract and retain visitors.
8. *Analytics*: Use analytics tools to track your website's performance, traffic, and revenue. This data can help you optimize your ad placement, content, and marketing strategies to improve revenue over time.

On average, most website owners can expect to earn anywhere from a few cents to a few dollars per click or impression, although this can vary widely depending on the niche and traffic levels of your website. Successful bloggers and website owners who generate significant traffic and engagement can earn tens of thousands of dollars or more per month in ad revenue.

Ad revenue can be somewhat unpredictable and is subject to fluctuations based on factors such as changes in ad rates or changes in website traffic. To maximize your earnings potential from ad revenue, it's important to focus on building a high-quality website with engaging content and a loyal audience, and to continually test and optimize your ad placements and types to maximize clicks and revenue.

Generating passive income through ad revenue from blogs and websites requires time and effort in creating high-quality content, attracting, and retaining a large audience, and optimizing the website for search engines and user experience. Once established, it can be a reliable source of passive income.

Creating and Selling Digital Art

In today's digital age, creating and selling digital art has become an increasingly popular way to generate passive income. With the rise of online marketplaces and the increasing demand for digital content, it has never been easier to turn your artistic talents into a profitable side hustle. This chapter will explore how to get started with creating and selling digital art, the different types of digital art, and the various platforms and resources available for artists to sell their work.

Before you can start selling digital art, you need to first create it. Digital art can take many forms, from illustrations and graphic designs to 3D renders and animations. It's important to find a style and medium that suits your skills and interests, as this will help you to create unique and original content that stands out from the crowd. There are many online resources available to help you get started with digital art, including tutorials, software, and courses.

Once you've created your digital art, it's time to start selling it. There are several online marketplaces and platforms that cater to digital art, including *Etsy*, *Creative Market*, and *Redbubble*. These platforms allow you to upload and sell your artwork, set your own prices, and earn a percentage of the sales. It's important to research each platform and choose the one that best suits your needs and goals.

To generate passive income from your digital art, you need to market it effectively. This can include promoting your artwork on social media, building an email list of potential customers, and collaborating with other artists or influencers. It's important to have a strong online presence and to showcase your work in a way that is visually appealing and engaging.

There are various free resources available to create digital art, some of which include:

1. *Krita* - a free and open-source digital painting software that offers a range of features to create professional-grade digital art.
2. *GIMP* - a free and open-source image editing software that can be used to create digital art.

3. *Canva* - a free graphic design platform that provides templates, graphics, and other design elements to create digital art for social media and marketing purposes.
4. *Inkscape* - a free and open-source vector graphics editor that can be used to create digital art, logos, and illustrations.
5. *Blender* - a free and open-source 3D creation software that can be used to create digital art, animations, and 3D models.

As with any form of art, copyright and legal considerations are important when creating and selling digital art. It's important to ensure that your work is original and not infringing on anyone else's intellectual property. You may also need to consider licensing and copyright laws when selling your artwork, particularly if you are using copyrighted materials or creating work for commercial use.

On average, most digital artists can expect to earn anywhere from a few hundred dollars to a few thousand dollars per month in profits, although this can vary widely depending on the popularity and visibility of your artwork. Successful digital artists who have built a strong following and established a recognizable brand can earn significant profits from selling their artwork, often earning tens of thousands of dollars or more per month.

Creating and selling digital art is an excellent way to generate passive income, particularly for those with a talent for art and design. With the right tools and resources, anyone can create and sell digital art, regardless of their skill level or experience. By following the tips and strategies outlined in this chapter, you can turn your passion for art into a profitable side hustle and start earning passive income today.

Building a Mobile Game

Building a mobile game can generate passive income through various channels such as in-app purchases, ads, and sponsorships. In-app purchases allow players to buy additional content, features, or virtual goods within the game. Ads are integrated into the game to display to players, and the game developer receives a share of the revenue from the ad network. Sponsorships are also possible by partnering with brands that want to reach the game's audience.

To create a mobile game, you can use game development engines such as *Unity*, *Unreal Engine*, or *GameMaker Studio*, which offer tools to create and deploy games on multiple platforms. You will also need skills in game design, programming, art, and sound to create a fun and engaging game.

Once you have created a mobile game, you can publish it on app stores such as Google Play or the Apple App Store, where players can download it for free or a fee. It's important to optimize your game's metadata, keywords, and screenshots to increase visibility and downloads.

To monetize your mobile game, you can offer in-app purchases such as extra lives, power-ups, or levels. You can also display ads within the game using ad networks such as *AdMob* or *Unity Ads*, which pay you based on the number of clicks or impressions. Additionally, you can consider sponsorships from companies that want to promote their products or services to your game's audience.

Building a successful mobile game requires a combination of creativity, technical skills, and marketing savvy. You need to create a game that stands out from the competition, has engaging gameplay, and offers a unique value proposition to players. You also need to promote your game through social media, influencers, and other marketing channels to reach a wide audience.

If building a mobile game yourself puts you outside of your comfort zone, there are several resources available to outsource its development. Here are some popular platforms:

1. *Upwork*: Upwork is a leading online marketplace that connects freelancers and clients from all over the world. It offers a vast pool of mobile game developers who can help you create a game from scratch or improve an existing game.
2. *Freelancer*: Freelancer is another popular platform where you can hire a mobile game developer. You can browse through the profiles of developers and choose the one that best suits your requirements.
3. *Fiverr*: Fiverr is a freelance platform that provides services for as low as $5. It has a category for game development services, where you can find freelancers who can build your mobile game.
4. *Toptal*: Toptal is a platform that specializes in connecting clients with the top 3% of freelance talent. It has a rigorous screening process for developers, ensuring you get the best talent to work on your project.
5. *Clutch*: Clutch is a B2B ratings and reviews platform that helps businesses find the best mobile app developers. It features verified reviews and ratings of developers, making it easier to find a reliable developer.
6. *Guru*: Guru is a freelance platform where you can find experienced mobile game developers. It offers features like project management tools, communication channels, and secure payment options.
7. *CodementorX*: CodementorX is a platform that connects businesses with pre-vetted developers. It has a pool of mobile game developers who can help you build your game.

Creating a mobile game can be a fun and potentially profitable way to generate passive income. However, there are several things you should be aware of before starting:

1. *Competition*: The mobile gaming market is highly competitive, and it can be challenging to stand out from the crowd. You need to research your competition and ensure that your game offers something unique and valuable that sets it apart.
2. *Development Costs*: Developing a mobile game can be expensive, and you need to have a budget for hiring developers, designers, and other professionals to help bring your game to life.

3. *App Store Optimization*: App Store Optimization (ASO) is critical for making your game discoverable and driving downloads. You need to research the right keywords, create an engaging app description, and optimize your app's icon and screenshots.
4. *Monetization Strategy*: There are several ways to monetize mobile games, including in-app purchases, advertising, and subscriptions. You need to determine the best monetization strategy for your game and implement it effectively.
5. *User Engagement*: User engagement is critical for retaining players and generating revenue. You need to ensure that your game is engaging, fun, and offers enough value to keep players coming back.
6. *Updates and Maintenance*: Mobile games require ongoing updates and maintenance to fix bugs, add new features, and keep up with changes in the industry. You need to have a plan for ongoing development and support.
7. *User Reviews*: User reviews are critical for driving downloads and improving your game's ranking in the app store. You need to encourage users to leave reviews and respond to feedback to improve your game over time.
8. *Legal Issues*: You need to comply with any legal requirements for developing and publishing a mobile game, such as copyright laws, privacy laws, and regulations governing in-app purchases.

On average, most mobile game developers can expect to earn anywhere from a few hundred dollars to a few thousand dollars per month in profits, although this can vary widely depending on the popularity and revenue model of the game. Successful mobile games that achieve high levels of downloads and engagement can earn significant profits, often earning tens or hundreds of thousands of dollars or more per month.

Building a mobile game can be a challenging but rewarding way to generate passive income, if you have the necessary skills, resources, and dedication to create and market a successful game.

Investing in Domain Names

Investing in domain names involves purchasing domain names with the intention of reselling them at a profit. This can generate passive income in two ways: first, by parking the domain names and earning advertising revenue from them, and second, by selling the domain names at a higher price than what was paid for them.

To generate passive income through parking, investors can use domain parking services, which place ads on the domain's landing page and generate revenue every time a user clicks on them. This method is particularly useful for high-traffic domain names.

To sell domain names at a profit, investors need to research and identify valuable domain names that are likely to be in high demand. This involves understanding domain name trends, search engine optimization, and market demand. Once a valuable domain name is identified, investors can purchase it and hold onto it until the market demand for it increases, at which point they can sell it at a higher price.

Investors can also participate in domain name auctions to acquire valuable domain names. Domain name auction sites such as *GoDaddy Auctions*, *NameJet*, and *Sedo* offer opportunities to bid on expired or previously registered domain names that may have a higher potential value.

To succeed in domain name investing, investors need to have a good understanding of the domain name market and be able to identify domain names with potential for high demand. They should also have a long-term investment strategy and be patient, as domain names may take time to appreciate in value.

Here are some additional resources to consider:

1. *GoDaddy Domain Name Appraisal*: This free tool can help you estimate the value of a domain name, giving you an idea of which names to purchase or hold onto for future investment.

2. *NamePros*: This is a popular domain name forum where you can learn more about the industry, connect with other investors, and even buy or sell domain names.

3. *DomainSherpa*: This website offers educational resources, interviews with industry experts, and a marketplace for buying and selling domain names.

4. *DomainInvesting.com*: This blog covers topics related to domain name investing, including buying & selling strategies, industry news, and trends to watch.

5. *ExpiredDomains.net*: This website provides a list of expired domains that are available for purchase, which can be a good way to acquire valuable names for a lower price.

6. *Google AdWords Keyword Planner*: This tool can help you research which keywords and phrases are popular among consumers, allowing you to choose domain names that are likely to generate traffic.

7. *Flippa*: This is an online marketplace where you can buy and sell websites, domain names, and other online assets. It can be a good resource for finding valuable domain names and connecting with potential buyers.

Investing in domain names can be a potentially lucrative way to generate passive income, but there are several things you should be aware of before starting:

1. *Market Trends*: Domain name values can fluctuate depending on market trends, so it's important to stay up to date on current trends and future projections to make informed investment decisions.

2. *Domain Name Quality*: The quality of the domain name can impact its value and potential for generating income. Premium domains that are short, memorable, and easy to spell are typically more valuable than long or complicated domain names.

3. *Domain Name Extensions*: Different domain name extensions, such as .com, .net, and .org, have different values and appeal to different audiences. .com is the most popular and valuable extension, but other extensions may be more appropriate for certain niches or industries.

4. ***Domain Name Acquisition***: You can acquire domain names through various methods, such as buying them from marketplaces, bidding in auctions, or reaching out to the current owner to negotiate a sale. It's important to have a budget and a strategy for acquiring domain names that align with your investment goals.

5. ***Domain Name Monetization***: There are several ways to monetize domain names, such as parking them with a domain parking service, selling them on marketplaces, or developing them into websites. It's important to choose the right monetization strategy based on the domain name's value and potential audience.

6. ***Legal Issues***: Domain name ownership can be complicated, and there are legal issues to be aware of, such as trademark infringement, cybersquatting, and domain name disputes. It's important to conduct due diligence and follow best practices to avoid legal issues.

7. ***Domain Name Renewal***: Domain names need to be renewed annually, and failure to do so can result in losing ownership of the domain. It's important to have a system in place for renewing domain names on time and managing your domain name portfolio effectively.

On average, most domain name investors can expect to earn anywhere from a few hundred dollars to a few thousand dollars per year in profits, although this can vary widely depending on the quality and marketability of the domain names they hold. Successful domain name investors who specialize in valuable and highly sought-after domain names can earn significant profits, often earning tens of thousands or hundreds of thousands of dollars or more per year.

By utilizing these resources, you can develop a solid strategy for investing in domain names and generating passive income. However, it's important to note that domain name investing can be a risky venture, and success is not guaranteed. It's important to thoroughly research each investment opportunity and be prepared to hold onto your domains for the long-term. investors should conduct proper due diligence before investing in any domain name and work with reputable domain name registrars and auction sites.

Chapter 4: Physical Products

Dropshipping

Dropshipping is a business model where an online retailer sells products to customers, but the retailer does not keep the products in stock. Instead, the retailer purchases the products from a third-party supplier who ships the product directly to the customer. This allows the retailer to avoid inventory costs and overhead associated with warehousing and shipping.

To generate passive income through dropshipping, the retailer sets up an online store, sources products from reliable suppliers, and markets the products to potential customers. When a customer places an order, the retailer purchases the product from the supplier and has it shipped directly to the customer. The retailer earns a profit by charging a markup on the product price.

One way to find reliable suppliers for dropshipping is to use online marketplaces such as *Alibaba* or *Oberlo*. These platforms allow retailers to browse a wide range of products and suppliers, and often offer tools to help manage orders and shipments.

To market the products and attract customers, retailers can use a variety of digital marketing techniques such as social media advertising, search engine optimization, and email marketing.

It's important for retailers to carefully research suppliers and product niches to ensure they are profitable and sustainable in the long term. Additionally, customer service and managing returns and refunds is a key aspect of dropshipping to maintain a positive reputation and ensure customer satisfaction.

There are several resources that can help you come up with ideas for dropshipping. Here are a few:

1. Trending Products: Use tools like *Google Trends*, *TrendHunter*, and *TrendWatching* to identify products that are currently popular or gaining popularity.

2. Social Media: Check out social media platforms like Instagram, Facebook, and Twitter to see what products influencers and users are sharing or talking about.

3. Competitor Analysis: Research your competitors to see what products they are selling and how they are marketing them. This can give you an idea of what is working in the market.

4. Marketplaces: Browse popular online marketplaces like *Amazon*, *eBay*, and *AliExpress* to see what products are in demand and how much they are selling for.

5. Niche Research: Identify a niche market that interests you and research products that cater to that market. You can use tools like *Google Keyword Planner*, *Google AdWords*, and *SEMrush* to help with your research.

6. *Product Hunt*: Product Hunt is a community-driven platform that showcases new and innovative products. You can use it to discover products that are gaining traction and might be good candidates for dropshipping.

7. Trade Shows: Attend trade shows in your industry to learn about new products and get inspiration for your dropshipping business.

8. *Spocket*: This is a dropshipping marketplace that allows you to find products from suppliers in the US and EU. It also offers fast shipping and branded invoicing.

9. *SaleHoo*: This is a directory of wholesalers and dropshippers that you can use to find products to sell. It also provides tools for market research and supplier verification.

10. *Google Trends*: This is a free tool that allows you to see the popularity of a product over time. It can help you identify products that are trending and have high demand.

11. *Facebook Ads Library*: This is a free tool that allows you to see the ads that your competitors are running. You can use this information to create effective ad campaigns for your dropshipping business.

12. *YouTube*: This is a great resource for learning about dropshipping. There are many channels and videos that offer tips and advice on how to succeed in this business.

On average, most dropshippers can expect to earn anywhere from a few hundred dollars to a few thousand dollars per month in profits, although this can vary widely depending on the quality of the products, the pricing strategy, and the marketing efforts.

Successful dropshippers who specialize in high-demand and unique products, use effective pricing and marketing strategies, and build a loyal customer base can earn significant profits, often earning tens of thousands of dollars or more per month.

Overall, dropshipping can be a lucrative source of passive income for those with an entrepreneurial spirit and a willingness to invest time and effort into building an online store and marketing it effectively. However, it does require a significant investment of time and resources to establish a successful store and generate consistent sales.

Amazon FBA

Amazon FBA (Fulfillment by Amazon) is a business model where you can sell your products on Amazon's online marketplace, and Amazon handles the fulfillment and shipping of your products. This means you can focus on sourcing products, marketing your listings, and growing your business without worrying about inventory management or shipping logistics.

To start an Amazon FBA business, you first need to find a profitable product niche and source products to sell. You can find suppliers on websites like Alibaba or AliExpress, and you can use tools *like Jungle Scout* or *Helium 10* to research product demand, competition, and profitability.

Once you have your products, you create a listing on Amazon's marketplace and send your inventory to Amazon's fulfillment centers. When a customer places an order, Amazon handles the picking, packing, and shipping of the product to the customer. Amazon also handles customer service and returns on your behalf.

To maximize your profits, it's important to optimize your listings with good product descriptions, high-quality images, and competitive pricing. You can also use Amazon's advertising platform to promote your listings and increase your sales.

Here are some free resources for Amazon FBA:

1. *Amazon Seller Central*: This is the main hub for Amazon FBA sellers. It provides a wealth of information on how to set up and manage your FBA account.
2. *Amazon FBA Help Center*: This is a comprehensive resource for getting answers to your questions about Amazon FBA. You can find detailed guides, videos, and webinars on a wide range of topics.
3. *Amazon Seller Forums*: This is a community of Amazon sellers who share tips, tricks, and advice on how to succeed with FBA. You can ask questions and get help from other sellers who have been through the same experiences.

4. *Jungle Scout*: This is a popular tool for Amazon FBA sellers. It provides market research data, sales estimates, and other useful information to help you find profitable products to sell.
5. *Helium 10*: This is another popular tool for Amazon FBA sellers. It provides keyword research, product research, and other features to help you optimize your listings and increase sales.
6. *YouTube*: There are many YouTube channels dedicated to Amazon FBA. You can find tutorials, interviews with successful sellers, and other useful content to help you succeed with FBA.
7. *Facebook Groups*: There are many Facebook groups dedicated to Amazon FBA. These groups provide a community of sellers who share tips, advice, and support.

On average, most Amazon FBA sellers can expect to earn anywhere from a few hundred dollars to a few thousand dollars per month in profits, although this can vary widely depending on the quality of the products, the pricing strategy, and the marketing efforts. Successful Amazon FBA sellers who specialize in high-demand and unique products, use effective pricing and marketing strategies, and build a loyal customer base can earn significant profits, often earning tens of thousands of dollars or more per month.

Amazon FBA can generate passive income because once your products are listed and your inventory is stocked, the process of fulfilling orders is handled by Amazon. This means you can earn money even when you're not actively working on your business. Additionally, Amazon's massive customer base and reputation can help drive sales and boost your profits. However, it's important to keep in mind that competition can be high, and there are fees associated with using Amazon's FBA service.

Print-on-Demand Products

Print on Demand (POD) products refer to a business model where a seller does not need to hold any inventory, but instead, products are printed or created as orders are placed by customers. Here are some ways that POD products can generate passive income:

1. Designing and selling T-shirts: You can use online platforms like *Teespring*, *Redbubble*, and *Merch by Amazon* to design and sell T-shirts. You upload your designs to the platform, and they take care of the printing and shipping. You earn a commission for each sale.
2. Creating and selling books: POD services like *Amazon's Kindle Direct Publishing* (KDP) and *IngramSpark* allow you to publish your own books, which are then printed and shipped when customers order them. You earn a royalty on each sale.
3. Designing and selling home decor items: POD companies like *Society6* and *Zazzle* allow you to design and sell products like wall art, throw pillows, and phone cases. You upload your designs, and the platform takes care of the printing and shipping. You earn a commission on each sale.
4. Creating and selling personalized products: POD services like *Printful* and *CustomCat* allow you to create and sell personalized products like mugs, phone cases, and bags. You upload your designs, and the platform takes care of the printing and shipping. You earn a commission on each sale.

Here are some popular free resources for Print on Demand products:

1. *Canva*: A free graphic design tool that you can use to create designs for your POD products.
2. *Printful*: A POD service that offers integrations with several e-commerce platforms like Shopify and WooCommerce.
3. *Kindle Direct Publishing*: A service that allows you to publish your own books on Amazon.
4. *Society6*: A POD platform that specializes in home decor items.

5. *Zazzle*: A POD platform that offers a wide range of customizable products.
6. *Redbubble*: A POD platform that allows you to sell your designs on a variety of products, including T-shirts, stickers, and posters.

On average, most print on demand sellers can expect to earn anywhere from a few hundred dollars to a few thousand dollars per month in profits, although this can vary widely depending on the quality of the products, the pricing strategy, and the marketing efforts.

Successful print on demand sellers who specialize in high-quality designs, use effective pricing and marketing strategies, and build a loyal customer base can earn significant profits, often earning tens of thousands of dollars or more per month.

Print on demand can be a lucrative source of passive income for those with a creative flair and a willingness to invest time and effort into designing and marketing profitable products.

Vending Machines

Vending machines offer a passive income stream by providing a convenient way for consumers to purchase products without the need for staff supervision. Once the machine is installed and stocked, it can generate income 24/7 without the need for ongoing maintenance. Vending machines can sell a wide variety of products, including snacks, drinks, and even electronics. By choosing the right products and locations, vending machines can generate a steady stream of passive income over time. Additionally, vending machines can be scaled easily by adding more machines in high-traffic areas, allowing for even greater earning potential.

Here are some free resources to get started with vending machines as a passive income source:

1. *National Automatic Merchandising Association* (NAMA) - This is the leading organization for the vending and refreshment services industry. They offer resources such as industry news, educational programs, and networking opportunities.
2. *VendingMarketWatch.com* - This website provides news, trends, and analysis for the vending industry. They also offer webinars and whitepapers on topics such as maximizing profits and reducing expenses.
3. *VendSoft* - This is a free vending machine management software that allows you to track inventory, sales, and profits from your machines.
4. *Vending World* - This website offers free guides on how to start a vending machine business and how to select the right machines and products for your business.
5. *Reddit* - There are several subreddits related to vending machines, such as *r/vendingmachines* and *r/vendingbusiness*, where you can ask questions and get advice from experienced vending machine operators.

There are several options for buying used vending machines, including online marketplaces such as *eBay*, *Craigslist*, and *Amazon*, as well as specialized vending machine dealers and auctions. It's important to thoroughly research and inspect the machine before purchasing to ensure its quality and functionality.

Here are some ways to find locations to place your vending machines:

1. *Ask local businesses*: Approach small businesses in your area such as gas stations, malls, offices, and ask if they would be interested in having a vending machine on their premises.
2. *Contact vending machine locators*: Vending machine locators are companies that specialize in finding locations for vending machines. You can hire them to find suitable locations for your vending machines.
3. *Use online resources*: There are online platforms that connect vending machine owners with businesses that are interested in having a vending machine on their premises. Some examples of such platforms include *VendSoft*, *Vending Connection*, and *VendLease*.
4. *Attend vending machine trade shows*: Trade shows are a great place to network with other vending machine operators and find out about potential locations for your vending machines.
5. *Conduct your own research*: Look around your local area for places that have high foot traffic, such as train stations, hospitals, and schools. These are all potential locations for vending machines.

Investing in vending machines can be a potentially profitable way to generate passive income, but there are several things you should be aware of before starting:

1. *Location*: The location of your vending machines is critical to their success. You need to research high-traffic areas and secure agreements with property owners or managers to place your machines.
2. *Machine Quality*: The quality and reliability of your vending machines can impact their success and longevity. It's important to invest in high-quality machines that are easy to operate and maintain.

3. ***Product Selection***: The products you offer in your vending machines can impact their success. You need to research customer preferences and select products that are in demand and have a good profit margin.
4. ***Pricing Strategy***: The pricing strategy for your vending machines can impact their profitability. You need to set prices that are competitive and profitable while also considering customer preferences and the cost of the products.
5. ***Maintenance and Restocking***: Vending machines require ongoing maintenance and restocking to ensure they are operating properly and have sufficient inventory. You need to have a plan for regular maintenance and restocking to keep your machines running smoothly.
6. ***Cash Management***: Vending machines generate cash, so you need to have a system in place for managing cash collection, counting, and depositing. It's important to have secure procedures to prevent theft or fraud.
7. ***Legal Issues***: Vending machines are subject to regulations and legal issues, such as health and safety requirements, licensing, and taxes. It's important to comply with all regulations and consult with legal and financial professionals as needed.

On average, a vending machine can generate between $20 to $300 per month in profit. However, this figure can fluctuate greatly depending on the location of the machine, as a machine located in a high-traffic area can generate more sales and profits than a machine in a low-traffic area.

Successful vending machine owners who choose high-traffic locations with a steady flow of customers, offer in-demand products at competitive prices, and provide good customer service can earn significant profits, often earning tens of thousands of dollars or more per year.

Vending machines can be a great source of passive income, by providing products to customers without requiring constant attention, allowing for flexibility and scalability in the business. Once established, a few hours a week is all that's needed to keep things running smoothly.

Affiliate Marketing

Affiliate marketing is the process of promoting other people's products and earning a commission for each sale made through your unique referral link. This can generate passive income as you can earn money while you sleep or do other activities once your affiliate links are set up and generating sales.

Here are some free resources for affiliate marketing:

1. *Affiliate Marketing Guide for Beginners by Neil Patel*: A comprehensive guide that covers everything you need to know about affiliate marketing, including finding affiliate programs, creating content, and driving traffic to your site.
2. *Affiliate Marketing Made Simple by Smart Passive Income*: A step-by-step guide that shows you how to start your own affiliate marketing business.
3. *Commission Junction*: A popular affiliate marketing network that allows you to find and join affiliate programs for a variety of products and services.
4. *Amazon Associates*: Amazon's affiliate marketing program that allows you to earn commissions on products sold through your affiliate links.
5. *ShareASale*: Another popular affiliate marketing network that offers a wide range of affiliate programs for bloggers and online marketers.
6. *ClickBank*: An affiliate marketing platform that specializes in digital products like eBooks, online courses, and software.
7. *Affiliate Marketing Forum by Warrior Forum*: A community of affiliate marketers where you can learn and share strategies and tactics for growing your affiliate marketing business.
8. *HubSpot Affiliate Marketing Resources*: HubSpot offers a variety of free resources for affiliate marketers, including webinars, ebooks, and blog posts.

9. ***Affiliate Marketing Tools by AffiliateWP***: A collection of free and paid tools to help you manage and optimize your affiliate marketing program.
10. ***Affilorama***: A comprehensive affiliate marketing training program that offers free and premium resources to help you learn and grow your affiliate marketing business.
11. ***Reddit.com***: Affiliate marketing on Reddit can be a powerful tool to generate passive income. There are several subreddits dedicated to affiliate marketing, such as ***r/Affiliatemarketing*** and ***r/Affiliatemarketing101***, where you can learn more about the industry and connect with other affiliate marketers. You can also join subreddits related to your niche and share your affiliate links in a non-spammy way. However, it's important to follow Reddit's guidelines and avoid self-promotion or spamming, as it can lead to account suspension or even a ban.

There are several ways to generate traffic to your website to increase your affiliate marketing sales:

1. Search engine optimization (SEO): Optimize your website for search engines to improve its visibility and ranking. Use relevant keywords in your content and meta tags, create quality content, and use internal and external linking.
2. Social media: Use social media platforms like ***Facebook***, ***Twitter***, ***Instagram***, and ***LinkedIn*** to promote your website and products. Share your content, engage with your audience, and use hashtags.
3. Email marketing: Build an email list and send regular newsletters to your subscribers. Offer exclusive deals and promotions to encourage clicks and sales.
4. Content marketing: Create informative and engaging content, such as blog posts, videos, podcasts, and infographics. Share your content on social media, email newsletters, and other online platforms.
5. Paid advertising: Use paid advertising methods, such as ***Google Ads***, ***Facebook Ads***, and ***Instagram Ads***, to target your audience and drive traffic to your website.

Assuming you have a significant audience and are promoting products with high commission rates, it is possible to earn a substantial passive income through affiliate marketing. Some affiliate marketers earn anywhere from a few hundred dollars to tens of thousands of dollars per month in commissions.

However, it is important to note that building an engaged audience and establishing trust with them takes time and effort. You need to create valuable content that resonates with your audience and promotes products that align with their interests and needs. It is not a get-rich-quick scheme, and success with affiliate marketing requires patience and persistence.

The amount you can make with affiliate marketing for passive income can vary widely based on the above factors. If you have a sizable audience and are promoting high-paying products that are relevant to your audience, it is possible to earn a significant passive income through affiliate marketing. Remember to always disclose your affiliate links and comply with the Federal Trade Commission (FTC) guidelines for affiliate marketing.

White-Labeling Products

White labeling products involves taking an existing product, putting your brand or label on it, and selling it as your own. This business model can generate passive income by leveraging existing products and brands to create your own without the need to invest in the development and manufacturing of new products. As a white labeler, you can focus on marketing and sales, leaving the production and logistics to the original manufacturer. This allows you to earn a profit margin without the need for extensive investment or management. Here are resources to consider:

1. *Alibaba*: Alibaba is a popular platform that connects manufacturers with businesses looking to white label products. You can browse products by category and get in touch with manufacturers directly.
2. *ThomasNet*: ThomasNet is a directory of manufacturers and suppliers in various industries. You can search for products to white label and find manufacturers who can help you with the process.
3. *Private Label University*: Private Label University is an online course that teaches you how to start a white label business. The course covers everything from finding the right products to marketing and selling them.
4. *Jungle Scout*: Jungle Scout is a product research tool that helps you find profitable products to white label. You can use it to analyze sales data, track trends, and identify popular products in your niche.
5. *Upwork*: Upwork is a platform that connects businesses with freelancers who can help with various tasks, including white labeling products. You can find freelancers with experience in sourcing products, negotiating with manufacturers, and handling logistics.

There are several ways to come up with ideas for white labeling products:

1. Identify a need: Look for gaps in the market where there is a demand for a particular product, but no one is currently providing

it. Conduct market research to understand consumer behavior and identify opportunities.

2. Research trends: Keep up to date with the latest trends in your industry or niche. Look for products that are currently popular or emerging trends that could be the next big thing.

3. Look at competitors: Check out what your competitors are offering and look for ways to improve on their products. Identify areas where you can add value or create a unique selling proposition.

4. Find a supplier: Browse through supplier directories or search for manufacturers in your niche. Contact suppliers to find out if they offer white label or private label services.

5. Brainstorm: Set aside time to brainstorm ideas with your team or by yourself. Write down all ideas, no matter how silly they may seem, and then narrow them down to the most promising ones.

There are many resources available to help you design a logo for your white-label product, including:

1. *Canva*: Canva is a free graphic design tool that allows you to create logos, business cards, and other design elements. It also offers paid options with more advanced features.

2. *LogoMaker*: LogoMaker is a free logo design tool that allows you to create a professional-looking logo in minutes. You can also download high-resolution files for a fee.

3. *Fiverr*: Fiverr is a freelance marketplace where you can hire a graphic designer to create your logo for you. Prices vary depending on the designer and the complexity of the project.

4. *99designs*: 99designs is a platform that connects businesses with freelance designers who can create logos, websites, and other design elements. Prices vary depending on the designer and the complexity of the project.

5. *Upwork*: Upwork is another freelance marketplace where you can find graphic designers to create your logo. You can set a budget for your project and review portfolios before hiring a designer.

6. *Freelancer*: Freelancer is a global freelance marketplace where you can find graphic designers to create your logo. You

can post a project and receive bids from designers or browse portfolios and hire a designer directly.

The amount of passive income generated from white label products can vary widely depending on the product, the pricing strategy, and the demand for the product. Here are some sample amounts of passive income that white label products can generate:

1. *Health and beauty products*: White labeling health and beauty products such as skincare, hair care, and supplements can generate anywhere from a few hundred to several thousand dollars per month in passive income.
2. *Apparel*: White labeling apparel such as t-shirts, hoodies, and hats can generate several hundred to several thousand dollars per month in passive income, depending on the pricing and the demand for the product.
3. *Electronics*: White labeling electronics such as headphones, speakers, and phone cases can generate several hundred to several thousand dollars per month in passive income, depending on the pricing and the demand for the product.
4. *Home goods*: White labeling home goods such as kitchen gadgets, pet products, and home decor can generate several hundred to several thousand dollars per month in passive income, depending on the pricing and the demand for the product.

Remember, when choosing a product to white label, ensure that it aligns with your brand and values, and that you can provide high-quality products that meet the needs of your target audience.

Wholesale Products

Wholesale products can be a lucrative source of passive income for entrepreneurs looking to create an online business or expand their existing one. By purchasing products in bulk from a supplier at a discounted price, and then selling them at a markup to consumers, you can generate significant profits without much ongoing effort.

One of the biggest advantages of wholesale products is that you can often sell them on various online marketplaces such as Amazon, eBay, or your own e-commerce store. You don't need to manufacture or create the products yourself, saving you time, money, and resources. You simply need to find the right products that are in demand, negotiate a good price with a reputable supplier, and then list them for sale online.

However, it's important to do your research and due diligence before diving into wholesale products. It's critical to choose the right products that have a proven track record of demand and profitability. You should also consider the competition and ensure that you can differentiate your product offering in the marketplace. Additionally, you need to have a solid marketing plan to attract potential customers to your online store or marketplace listing.

Another key consideration is finding the right supplier for your wholesale products. You need to ensure that they have a good reputation, offer high-quality products, and can reliably fulfill your orders. It's also important to negotiate favorable terms, such as minimum order quantities, shipping costs, and delivery times, to maximize your profits.

There are several ways to find wholesale products for sale:

1. *Online wholesale marketplaces*: There are several online marketplaces that connect wholesale suppliers with buyers. Some popular examples include *Alibaba*, *DHgate*, and *Global Sources*.
2. *Trade shows*: Attending trade shows can be a great way to connect with wholesale suppliers and view their products in person. Trade shows are typically held in large convention centers and are open to industry professionals.

3. ***Wholesale directories***: There are several directories that list wholesale suppliers in various industries. Some popular examples include ***Wholesale Central, SaleHoo***, and ***Worldwide Brands***.
4. ***Directly contacting manufacturers***: If you have a specific product in mind, you can reach out to the manufacturer directly and inquire about their wholesale pricing and terms.
5. ***Referrals***: Ask other business owners or industry professionals if they have any recommendations for wholesale suppliers in your industry.

Investing in wholesale products can be a potentially profitable way to generate passive income, but there are several things you should be aware of before starting:

1. ***Product Research***: The products you choose to sell are critical to the success of your business. You need to research market trends, customer demand, and competition to select products with good profit margins and long-term potential.
2. ***Supplier Selection***: The quality and reliability of your suppliers can impact your profitability and customer satisfaction. You need to research suppliers and choose ones that offer high-quality products, competitive pricing, and reliable delivery.
3. ***Inventory Management***: Inventory management is critical to the success of your business. You need to have a system in place for tracking inventory levels, ordering products on time, and managing stock to avoid overstocking or understocking.
4. ***Pricing Strategy***: The pricing strategy for your products can impact their profitability and customer appeal. You need to set prices that are competitive and profitable while also considering customer preferences and the cost of the products.
5. ***Marketing and Sales***: Marketing and sales are essential to the success of your business. You need to have a plan for promoting your products, reaching your target audience, and building a customer base.
6. ***Shipping and Handling***: Shipping and handling can impact your customer satisfaction and profitability. You need to have a system

in place for shipping products on time, managing returns and exchanges, and handling customer inquiries.

7. *Legal Issues*: Wholesale products are subject to regulations and legal issues, such as licensing, taxes, and import/export requirements. It's important to comply with all regulations and consult with legal and financial professionals as needed.

Profit margins for wholesale products can vary widely depending on the specific product, the market demand, and the pricing strategy. To achieve high profit margins with wholesale products, it is important to conduct thorough research, negotiate with suppliers for the best prices, and develop effective marketing strategies to reach your target audience and drive sales. Some wholesale products that typically have higher profit margins include:

1. *Clothing and accessories*: Clothing and accessories, such as hats, jewelry, and bags, often have high profit margins due to their relatively low cost of production and high perceived value.

2. *Electronics*: Electronic products, such as headphones, phone cases, and charging cables, can also have high profit margins if you are able to source them at a good price and sell them effectively.

3. *Health and wellness products*: Health and wellness products, such as supplements, vitamins, and workout equipment, can also have high profit margins due to the growing interest in health and wellness.

4. *Home goods*: Home goods, such as kitchen gadgets, bedding, and decor, can also have high profit margins due to the perceived value and relatively low cost of production.

The amount of passive income you can expect to earn from wholesale products can range from a few hundred dollars per month to several thousand dollars per month or more, depending on the number of products you sell, and the profit margins you are able to achieve.

Success with wholesale products for passive income requires effective marketing, competitive pricing, and high-quality products that meet the needs of your target audience. With careful planning and execution, wholesale products can be a profitable source of passive income.

Licensing Your Inventions

Licensing your inventions can be an effective way to generate passive income. When you license your invention, you grant someone else the right to produce and sell your product in exchange for a royalty payment. This means that you don't have to invest your own money or time into manufacturing, marketing, and selling your invention, and can instead collect a percentage of the revenue from sales.

To license your invention, you first need to conduct a patent search to make sure your invention is original and doesn't infringe on any existing patents. Once you have established that your invention is unique, you can file a patent application with the US Patent and Trademark Office (USPTO) to protect your intellectual property.

Next, you can start looking for potential licensees by attending industry trade shows, networking with professionals in your field, and using online databases to find companies that may be interested in your invention. You can also hire a licensing agent or attorney to help you negotiate a licensing agreement that is fair and protects your interests.

Once you have found a licensee, you will negotiate the terms of the licensing agreement, including the royalty payment and any upfront fees. You may also need to provide the licensee with technical support, such as training or consulting, to help them manufacture and market your product effectively.

There are many resources available to help inventors develop and market their inventions. Here are a few:

1. *United States Patent and Trademark Office* (USPTO): The USPTO offers a wealth of information for inventors, including patent search tools, patent application resources, and information on intellectual property law.
2. *InventHelp*: InventHelp is an invention assistance company that provides a variety of services to help inventors develop and market their inventions. These services include patent referral services, prototyping, and marketing assistance.

3. *Edison Nation*: Edison Nation is a product innovation company that works with inventors to develop and market their inventions. They offer a variety of services, including product design and development, prototyping, and marketing.
4. *National Inventors Hall of Fame*: The National Inventors Hall of Fame is a non-profit organization that honors inventors and promotes innovation. They offer a variety of educational programs and resources for inventors, including workshops and invention competitions.
5. *SCORE*: SCORE is a non-profit organization that provides mentoring and resources to entrepreneurs and small business owners. They offer a variety of resources for inventors, including workshops and one-on-one mentoring.
6. *Inventors Digest*: Inventors Digest is a magazine and online resource for inventors. They offer a variety of articles, resources, and tools for inventors, including information on patents, licensing, and product development.
7. *Kickstarter* and *Indiegogo*: Crowdfunding platforms like Kickstarter and Indiegogo can be a great way for inventors to raise funds and test the market for their inventions. These platforms allow inventors to showcase their products and raise money from supporters in exchange for rewards or equity.
8. *Licensing Executives Society* (LES): LES is a professional organization for licensing executives and professionals. They offer a variety of resources and educational programs for inventors and entrepreneurs, including licensing workshops and networking events.

Licensing your inventions can be a potentially profitable way to generate passive income, but there are several things you should be aware of before starting:

1. *Protecting Your Intellectual Property*: Before licensing your inventions, it's important to protect your intellectual property through patents, trademarks, or copyrights. This can help prevent others from copying or using your inventions without permission.

2. *Researching the Market*: You need to research the market and industry trends to determine if there is a demand for your invention. This can help you determine if licensing your invention is a viable option.

3. *Negotiating Licensing Agreements*: You need to negotiate licensing agreements with potential licensees. This can include determining the terms of the license, the royalty rate, and the duration of the agreement.

4. *Monitoring Your Licensees*: Once you have licensed your invention, it's important to monitor your licensees to ensure they are complying with the terms of the agreement. This can include monitoring sales, collecting royalties, and enforcing any patents or trademarks.

5. *Legal Issues*: Licensing your inventions can be subject to legal issues, such as licensing agreements, patents, and intellectual property disputes. It's important to consult with legal and financial professionals as needed to protect your interests.

Typically, licensing rates for inventions range from 2% to 10% of the net sales of the licensed product. However, some licensing agreements may include a flat fee or a combination of a flat fee and a royalty percentage.

It's important to note that the licensing rate is not the only factor that determines the potential earnings from licensing your invention. The market demand, the quality of the licensed product, and the marketing and distribution strategies of the licensee can also affect the amount of passive income you earn from licensing your invention.

Licensing your inventions can be a lucrative way to generate passive income, especially if your invention is innovative and in demand. It allows you to earn money without having to invest in production or marketing and can provide a steady stream of revenue for years to come.

Creating a Product and Selling on Amazon

Creating a product and selling on Amazon is an excellent way to generate passive income. With the help of Amazon's extensive customer base and fulfillment network, you can easily reach a large audience and generate consistent sales.

To start, you need to come up with a product idea that solves a problem or meets a need. You can then source the product, either by manufacturing it yourself or finding a supplier, and create a listing on Amazon. Amazon offers tools to help you optimize your listing, including product descriptions, images, and pricing.

Here are some strategies to help you find high demand, low competition items to sell on Amazon:

1. *Use Amazon's Best Seller Rank*: Amazon's Best Seller Rank (BSR) is a good indicator of a product's popularity. Look for products with a BSR of less than 5,000 in their category, as this indicates that they sell well on Amazon.

2. *Analyze customer reviews*: Analyzing customer reviews can give you an idea of what customers are looking for and what products they are dissatisfied with. Look for products that have high demand but also have a large number of negative reviews or low ratings, as this may indicate an opportunity to improve upon the product.

3. *Use Amazon Product Research Tools*: There are several tools available that can help you identify products that have high demand and low competition. Tools such as *Jungle Scout, Helium 10*, and *AMZScout* can provide insights into product sales data, competition, and other valuable metrics to help you make informed decisions about what products to sell on Amazon.

4. *Check out Amazon's "Movers and Shakers"*: Amazon's "Movers and Shakers" page highlights products that have experienced a significant increase in sales rank over the past 24 hours. This can

be a good indicator of products that are trending or have sudden popularity.

5. *Niche down:* Instead of trying to compete in highly competitive categories such as electronics or apparel, consider niching down to a smaller subcategory. This can help you identify products that are in high demand but have less competition.

Once your product is listed, Amazon will handle the fulfillment process, including shipping and customer service. All you need to do is monitor your sales and adjust as needed.

According to a 2020 survey conducted by *Jungle Scout*, a software platform for Amazon sellers, the median annual revenue for Amazon sellers in the US is $60,000. However, this number can vary widely based on several factors, such as the product category, competition, and marketing and sales strategies employed by the seller. Some Amazon sellers generate only a few hundred dollars per month in revenue, while others earn tens or hundreds of thousands of dollars per month. Having a unique or high-demand product, effective marketing and advertising strategies, competitive pricing, and strong customer service can all affect how much you make.

Selling on Amazon also comes with expenses, such as Amazon fees, shipping costs, and inventory storage fees, which can impact overall profitability. Additionally, selling on Amazon requires ongoing effort to manage product listings, monitor competition, and adjust marketing and sales strategies to remain competitive.

There are many resources available to help you create and sell products on Amazon, including Amazon's own resources, such as their Seller Central platform and Amazon Advertising. Additionally, there are many third-party tools and services, such as product research tools and Amazon consulting services, that can help you optimize your sales and generate more passive income.

Selling on Etsy or Other Handmade Marketplaces

Selling on Etsy or other handmade marketplaces can generate passive income by creating and selling handmade items, digital downloads, and vintage goods. It is a platform where artisans, crafters, and creators can sell their products to a global audience without worrying about the hassles of building their own website and driving traffic to it.

One of the biggest benefits of selling on Etsy or other handmade marketplaces is that it provides a ready-made audience that is interested in handmade and unique products. This audience is actively seeking out items that are not mass-produced, which makes it easier to attract potential buyers.

Sellers can create a passive income stream by creating unique and in-demand products that can be replicated and sold multiple times. They can also create digital products like patterns or printable art that can be downloaded and sold multiple times with little to no additional effort.

Another advantage of selling on Etsy or other handmade marketplaces is that they handle the technical aspects of the transaction, such as payment processing and shipping. This allows sellers to focus on creating and listing their products without worrying about the logistics of running an online store.

There are many resources available for sellers on Etsy or other handmade marketplaces, including tutorials on how to set up a shop, how to optimize listings, and how to market products. Additionally, many sellers on these platforms are willing to share their experiences and provide tips and advice to help others succeed.

There are several alternatives to Etsy for selling handmade goods and crafts online. Some popular options include:

1. ***Handmade at Amazon***: Amazon's own marketplace for handcrafted items. It has a similar fee structure to Etsy, with a 15% referral fee on sales.
2. ***ArtFire***: Another online marketplace for handmade and vintage items, with lower fees than Etsy (12.75% commission on sales).
3. ***Zibbet***: A platform for independent artists and makers to sell their handmade items, with no listing fees and a flat monthly fee.
4. ***Folksy***: A UK-based marketplace for handmade goods, with low listing fees and a 6% commission on sales.
5. ***Aftcra***: A marketplace exclusively for American handmade goods, with a focus on supporting small businesses and local artisans.
6. ***Handmadeology Market***: A marketplace created by the Handmadeology blog, featuring handmade and vintage items.
7. ***Cratejoy***: A subscription box marketplace that allows makers to sell their own curated subscription boxes.

Selling on Etsy or other handmade product websites can be a potentially profitable way to generate passive income, but there are several things you should be aware of before starting:

1. ***Product Quality***: The quality of your handmade products can impact customer satisfaction and repeat business. You need to have a system in place for quality control to ensure your products meet your standards.
2. ***Product Listing***: Your product listing should be clear, informative, and attractive. You need to provide accurate descriptions, high-quality images, and relevant tags and categories to help customers find your products.
3. ***Pricing Strategy***: The pricing strategy for your handmade products can impact their profitability and customer appeal. You need to set prices that are competitive and profitable while also considering customer preferences and the cost of materials and labor.
4. ***Marketing and Sales***: Marketing and sales are essential to the success of your business. You need to have a plan for promoting your products, reaching your target audience, and building a customer base.

5. ***Customer Service***: Good customer service is critical to building a positive reputation and repeat business. You need to have a system in place for responding to customer inquiries, addressing issues, and providing timely and accurate order fulfillment.
6. ***Shipping and Handling***: Shipping and handling is a critical component of selling on Etsy or other handmade product websites. You need to have a system in place for managing orders, shipping products on time, and handling customer inquiries.
7. ***Legal Issues***: Selling handmade products online is subject to regulations and legal issues, such as taxes, licensing, and product liability. It's important to comply with all regulations and consult with legal and financial professionals as needed.

The average income of an Etsy seller varies widely depending on factors such as the type of products sold, the seller's experience, and their marketing efforts. However, according to a survey conducted by Etsy in 2020, the average annual revenue for Etsy sellers was around $10,000 USD.

It's worth noting that this figure may not represent the earnings of all Etsy sellers, as some sellers may earn significantly more or less than this amount. Some successful Etsy sellers have reported earning six-figure incomes, while others may struggle to make a significant profit.

To increase your chances of making a good income as an Etsy seller, it's important to focus on creating high-quality products, optimizing your listings with great photos and descriptions, and providing excellent customer service. Building a strong brand and marketing your products effectively can also help to increase your sales and profitability.

Selling on Etsy or other handmade marketplaces can be a great way to generate passive income by creating and selling unique, handmade products and digital downloads to a global audience. With the right products and marketing strategies, it is possible to create a successful and sustainable business on these platforms.

Chapter 5: Rental Opportunities

Rent Out a Room in Your House

Renting out a room in your house is a popular way to generate passive income. By renting out a room, you can earn extra money each month without having to do much work. It's a great way to make use of extra space in your home and generate income without having to take on a second job.

To get started with renting out a room in your house, you'll need to make sure you have a space that's suitable for guests. This may mean decluttering and cleaning the room, making sure it's well-lit and comfortable, and providing any necessary amenities like fresh linens and towels.

Next, you'll need to determine how much to charge for the room. You can do this by researching similar listings in your area and setting a competitive price. You'll also want to create a listing on a platform like *Airbnb* or *VRBO* to make it easy for potential guests to find your space.

Once you've set up your listing, you'll need to manage bookings and communicate with guests. This can be done through the platform's messaging system, and you may need to coordinate check-ins and provide any necessary instructions or information about your home.

Here are some resources for renting out a room in your home beyond Airbnb & VRBO:

1. *Craigslist*: Craigslist is a free classified ads website that can be used to advertise your room for rent. They have a "Rooms & Shares" section where you can post your listing.
2. *Roommates.com*: Roommates.com is a website that helps you find roommates and rent out a room in your home. They offer a range of resources for landlords, including background checks and lease agreements.
3. *Zillow*: Zillow is primarily a real estate website, but they also offer resources for landlords who are looking to rent out a spare room. They have a "Rentals" section where you can list your room for rent.

4. *Facebook Groups*: Facebook has a range of local groups where you can advertise your room for rent. Look for groups in your area that focus on housing or roommates.
5. *HomeAway*: HomeAway is a platform that specializes in vacation rentals, but you can also use it to rent out a room in your home. They offer resources for hosts, including a blog with hosting tips.
6. *Your local government*: Check with your local government to see if they have any resources for landlords. Some cities offer resources such as landlord-tenant guides and rental assistance programs.

The amount of passive income you can earn by renting out a room in your house will depend on various factors, such as your location, the size and condition of the room, and the demand for rental properties in your area. However, according to data from Zillow, the average monthly rent for a spare room in a U.S. home is around $530 USD.

Of course, the amount you can charge for a room in your house may be higher or lower than this average depending on your location and other factors. It's important to research rental prices in your area to get a better idea of what you can charge.

While renting out a room can be a great way to earn passive income, it's important to keep in mind any local laws or regulations related to short-term rentals. You'll also want to make sure you're prepared for any potential issues that may arise with guests, such as noise complaints or damages to your home. Overall, renting out a room can be a great way to earn extra income with minimal effort if you're prepared and responsible as a host.

Rent Out Your Car on Turo

Renting out your car on Turo is a form of peer-to-peer car sharing where car owners can rent out their vehicles to people in need of transportation. This is a viable way to generate passive income as you don't have to do anything after setting up your car listing, except approve or reject rental requests.

To get started with Turo, you'll need to create an account and list your car. The process involves taking photos of your car, setting your rental rates, and writing a description of your car. Turo has a pricing tool that can help you set your rental rates based on your car's make, model, and location. It's also important to set up a convenient meeting place to exchange the car keys with renters.

Turo provides liability insurance up to $1 million, which means you don't have to worry about covering damages to your vehicle. They also offer a screening process for renters to ensure that they have a valid driver's license and a clean driving record.

To increase your rental income, you can offer additional services like airport pickup and drop off or provide a discount for renters who rent your car for an extended period. Additionally, keeping your car in good condition and responding promptly to rental requests can help you earn positive reviews, which can increase your chances of getting more rentals in the future.

There are several alternatives to Turo, and It's important to research each platform to determine which one is the best fit for your needs and location. Alternatives include:

1. *Getaround*: This platform lets you rent your car to people in your community on an hourly or daily basis.
2. *Zipcar*: Zipcar allows car owners to rent out their cars by the hour or day to people who need a vehicle for a short period of time.
3. *Hyrecar*: Hyrecar is a peer-to-peer car rental marketplace that connects car owners with rideshare drivers who need a vehicle to drive for companies like Uber and Lyft.

4. *Maven*: Maven is a car-sharing platform that lets car owners rent out their vehicles to people in their area for short-term use.
5. Turo alternatives: Other similar car-sharing platforms to Turo include *Car Next Door*, *Drivy*, and *Hiyacar*.

The amount of passive income you can earn by renting out your car on Turo will depend on various factors, such as the make and model of your car, its age and condition, your location, and the demand for rental cars in your area. According to Turo, hosts on their platform can earn an average of $706 USD per month, but this can vary widely depending on the factors mentioned above.

To get a better idea of how much you could earn by renting out your car on Turo, you can use Turo's carculator tool on their website. This tool considers factors such as your car's make and model, year, location, and availability, and provides an estimate of how much you could earn per day and per month.

It's worth noting that renting out your car on Turo will require some initial investment in terms of preparing your car for renters and ensuring that it meets Turo's safety and quality standards. You will also need to consider any additional expenses such as insurance, maintenance, and cleaning services.

Overall, renting out your car on Turo can be a good way to earn some extra passive income, but it's important to carefully consider all the factors involved and ensure that you are comfortable with having someone else drive your car. It's also a viable option for people who have an extra car that they don't use frequently.

Rent Out Storage Space

Renting out storage space can be a great way to generate passive income. There are several options for renting out storage space, including self-storage units, garage space, and even spare rooms in your home. By renting out your unused storage space, you can earn extra money without much effort on your part.

One option for renting out storage space is to use a self-storage facility. These facilities provide secure and climate-controlled storage units that renters can use to store their belongings. You can rent out a unit or multiple units at the facility to earn passive income.

Another option is to rent out garage space or a spare room in your home for storage. This can be a great option for those who don't have a self-storage facility nearby or who want to provide a more personalized storage experience. You can advertise your storage space on online platforms or through local classifieds to find renters.

Additionally, there are online platforms like **Neighbor** and **StoreAtMyHouse** that allow you to rent out your storage space to others in your area. These platforms handle the rental process for you, making it a convenient way to earn passive income from your unused storage space.

Here are some alternatives to Neighbor and StoreAtMyHouse you can use:

1. *Spacer*: Spacer is an online marketplace that connects people who need storage space with those who have extra space to rent. They handle payments, contracts, and insurance, making the process easy for you.
2. *Craigslist*: Craigslist is a popular online classifieds site where you can list your storage space for rent. You'll need to manage the process yourself, but it can be a good way to find local renters.
3. *Facebook Marketplace*: Facebook Marketplace is a popular platform for buying and selling items, but you can also use it to list your storage space for rent. It's a good way to reach a large audience in your local area.

4. **Sparefoot**: Sparefoot is an online marketplace that connects people who need storage space with those who have extra space to rent. They handle payments, contracts, and insurance, making the process easy for you.
5. **Your local self-storage facilities**: If you don't want to manage the process yourself, you can also check with your local self-storage facilities to see if they offer rental options for extra space. They may handle the process for you and pay you a percentage of the rental fees.

The amount of passive income you can earn by renting out storage space on these platforms will depend on various factors, such as the location and size of the space, the demand for storage in your area, and the rental prices of similar storage units in your area.

According to data from Neighbor, hosts on their platform earn an average of $156 USD per month for a 10'x10' storage space, but this can vary widely depending on the factors mentioned above.

To get a better idea of how much you could earn by renting out your storage space, you can research rental prices for similar storage units in your area and set your rental price accordingly. It's also important to consider any additional expenses such as insurance, maintenance, and cleaning services.

Remember to do your research and carefully read the terms and conditions of any platform or service before listing your storage space for rent. It's important to carefully consider all the factors involved and ensure that you are comfortable with renting out your storage space to others. With the right preparation and marketing, renting out storage space can be a lucrative passive income stream.

Rent Out Office Space

Renting out office space can be a lucrative source of passive income, especially if you have extra space in your commercial property or home office. By renting out your extra space, you can earn a steady stream of income without much effort on your part.

Here are a few things to consider before getting started:

1. Zoning laws: Make sure you check your local zoning laws to ensure that you're allowed to rent out office space in your home. Some areas have restrictions on what types of businesses can operate in residential areas.
2. Insurance: You'll need to have the proper insurance coverage for your home and office space. Talk to your insurance provider to find out what coverage you'll need.
3. Permits and licenses: Depending on where you live, you may need to obtain permits and licenses before you can rent out office space in your home.
4. Safety and security: You'll need to ensure that your home office space is safe and secure for your tenants. This may include installing security cameras, adding locks to doors and windows, and making sure there are no hazards that could cause accidents.
5. Privacy: Consider how you'll maintain your privacy and personal space while renting out office space in your home. You may want to set boundaries around when and how your tenants can access certain areas of your home.
6. Lease agreement: It's important to have a clear and comprehensive lease agreement in place that outlines the terms and conditions of renting out your office space. This can help avoid misunderstandings and conflicts down the road.

To start, you can list your office space for rent on various online marketplaces such as *Craigslist*, *LoopNet*, and *CoStar*. These platforms allow you to create an advertisement for your space, set the price, and connect with potential renters. You can also consider working with a commercial real estate broker or property management company to help you find and manage tenants. They can assist with lease agreements, rent collection, and maintenance issues, saving you time and hassle.

Another option is to list your space on coworking websites like **Desktime**, **ShareDesk**, or **LiquidSpace**. These websites connect freelancers and small businesses with office space owners, giving you access to a broader pool of potential renters.

The amount of passive income you can earn by renting out storage space will depend on several factors, such as the size and location of the storage space, the demand for storage in your area, and the rental prices of similar storage units in your area.

According to data from platforms such as **Neighbor** and **StoreAtMyHouse**, hosts can earn anywhere from $50 to $500 per month by renting out their storage space. However, this can vary widely depending on the factors mentioned above.

To get a better idea of how much you could earn by renting out your storage space, you can research rental prices for similar storage units in your area and set your rental price accordingly. It's also important to consider any additional expenses such as insurance, maintenance, and cleaning services.

With proper management and maintenance, renting out office space can generate a steady stream of passive income that can help supplement your income and grow your wealth.

Rent Out Equipment Such as Cameras, Microphones, And Other Audio and Video Equipment

Renting out equipment, such as cameras, microphones, and other audio and video equipment, can be an excellent way to generate passive income. Many people need equipment for various projects, but they don't want to invest in the equipment themselves. By renting out your equipment, you can provide a valuable service and earn income without much effort.

To start, make an inventory of your equipment and decide which items you are willing to rent out. Determine the rental rates and policies, such as rental duration, deposit requirements, and liability issues. You can advertise your equipment rental services online through social media, classifieds websites, or local listings. You can also partner with production companies or event planners who may need your equipment for their projects.

To ensure that your equipment is always in good condition, it is important to maintain and clean it regularly. You may also want to consider investing in insurance coverage to protect your equipment from any damage or loss.

Renting out equipment can also provide networking opportunities and lead to future business opportunities. It is a great way to build relationships with clients and develop a positive reputation in your industry.

Don't own any equipment? Here's where you can source cameras, microphones, and other audio & video equipment affordably:

1. *eBay*: eBay is a popular online marketplace where you can find used equipment at affordable prices.
2. *Craigslist*: Craigslist is an online classifieds website where you can find used equipment being sold by individuals in your local area.

3. *Facebook Marketplace*: Facebook Marketplace is another online marketplace where you can find used equipment being sold by individuals in your local area.
4. *B&H Used Department*: B&H is a popular retailer for new and used camera equipment. Their used department offers a wide selection of used equipment at discounted prices.
5. *KEH*: KEH is another popular retailer for used camera equipment. They offer a large selection of used equipment and provide a 180-day warranty on most items.
6. *Adorama Used Department*: Adorama is another popular retailer for new and used camera equipment. Their used department offers a wide selection of used equipment at discounted prices.
7. *Local camera shops*: Local camera shops may also offer used equipment at affordable prices. It's worth checking out the shops in your area.

There are several websites where you can rent out your cameras, microphones, and other audio and video equipment to others. Here are a few popular options:

1. *ShareGrid* - ShareGrid is a peer-to-peer rental marketplace that connects filmmakers and photographers with gear owners. It's available in several major cities in the US, including Los Angeles, New York, and Chicago.
2. *KitSplit* - KitSplit is another peer-to-peer rental platform for photographers and filmmakers. It allows you to rent out everything from cameras and lenses to lighting and audio equipment.
3. *LensRentals* - LensRentals is a rental service that specializes in camera gear. They offer a wide range of equipment, including cameras, lenses, and accessories, and they ship nationwide in the US.
4. *Fat Llama* - Fat Llama is a platform that allows you to rent out all kinds of items, including cameras and audio equipment. It's available in several countries, including the US, UK, and Canada.
5. *CameraLends* - CameraLends is a rental service that specializes in cameras and lenses. It's available in several major cities in the US, including Los Angeles, San Francisco, and New York.

6. **BorrowLenses** - BorrowLenses is a rental service that offers cameras, lenses, and other equipment for photographers and videographers. They ship nationwide in the US.

The amount of passive income you can earn by renting out audio and video equipment will depend on several factors, such as the type and quality of the equipment, the demand for equipment rentals in your area, and the rental prices of similar equipment in your area.

According to data from platforms such as **ShareGrid** and **Fat Llama**, hosts can earn anywhere from $50 to $500 per day by renting out audio and video equipment. However, this can vary widely depending on the factors mentioned above.

To get a better idea of how much you could earn by renting out your audio and video equipment, you can research rental prices for similar equipment in your area and set your rental price accordingly. It's also important to consider any additional expenses such as insurance, maintenance, and cleaning services.

Before purchasing any used equipment, it's important to research the seller and thoroughly inspect the equipment to ensure that it is in good working condition. Overall, renting out equipment can be a profitable and low-effort way to generate passive income. By providing a valuable service to others, you can earn income while your equipment is put to good use.

Rent Out Parking Spaces

Renting out parking spaces is a great way to generate passive income for those who have unused parking spaces. This can be in the form of a garage, driveway, or even a vacant lot. By renting out your parking space, you can earn money without having to do much work.

One way to rent out your parking space is by listing it on online marketplaces such as *Parkopedia*, *SpotHero*, or *JustPark*. These websites allow you to list your parking space for free and connect you with people who need a place to park. You can set your own prices, availability, and any other requirements you have.

Another option is to rent out your parking space to individuals or businesses in your area. You can do this by advertising your parking space on social media, local classified ads, or even putting up a sign outside your property. This method may require more effort in terms of finding interested parties, but it can also result in a higher profit margin.

Renting out parking spaces can be a great way to generate passive income, but it's important to be aware of some key considerations before getting started. Here are some things to keep in mind:

1. *Local regulations*: Check with your local zoning and land use authorities to ensure that you are legally allowed to rent out parking spaces in your area. Some areas may require permits or have specific zoning laws for parking rental businesses.
2. *Liability and insurance*: As the property owner, you may be held liable for any accidents or damage that occurs on your property. It's important to make sure you have adequate insurance coverage and liability protection in case of any incidents.
3. *Maintenance and upkeep*: You will need to maintain the parking spaces to ensure they are safe and clean for your customers. This may include repairing potholes, sweeping & cleaning the area, and ensuring proper lighting.
4. *Payment and billing*: Determine how you will collect rent and manage payments from customers. You may choose to use a

service like PayPal or Stripe to manage payments or handle it manually through invoicing and bank transfers.

5. ***Customer management***: Consider how you will handle customer inquiries, complaints, and disputes. You may need to establish clear guidelines and policies for how customers can access the parking spaces, what happens if they are late on payments, and what your refund policy is.

6. Marketing and advertising: Think about how you will market and advertise your parking spaces to potential customers. You may choose to list them on online marketplaces like Craigslist or Airbnb, or use social media and other advertising channels to promote your rental business. The amount of passive income you can earn by renting out parking spaces will depend on several factors, such as the location of the parking space, the demand for parking in your area, and the rental prices of similar parking spaces in your area.

According to data from platforms such as ***Parkable***, ***JustPark***, and ***SpotHero***, hosts can earn anywhere from $50 to $300 per month by renting out parking spaces. However, this can vary widely depending on the factors mentioned above.

To get a better idea of how much you could earn by renting out your parking space, you can research rental prices for similar parking spaces in your area and set your rental price accordingly. It's also important to consider any additional expenses such as maintenance and cleaning services.

Overall, renting out parking spaces can be a profitable and relatively low-effort way to generate passive income, especially for those living in high-demand urban areas where parking is at a premium.

Rent Out Boats or Other Recreational Vehicles

Renting out boats and other recreational vehicles can be a great way to generate passive income. Many people enjoy boating and RV trips, but not everyone has the money or desire to buy their own equipment. This creates an opportunity for owners to rent out their boats, RVs, and other recreational vehicles to those looking for a fun and affordable way to enjoy the outdoors.

There are several benefits to renting out boats and RVs. For one, the initial investment cost is usually lower than other forms of real estate or equipment rental. Additionally, the rental prices can be quite high, especially during peak seasons or holidays, allowing owners to generate a significant amount of passive income. Finally, owners can choose to rent out their equipment through various platforms and websites, making it easy to find and manage renters.

To get started, owners will need to invest in high-quality equipment and ensure that it is properly maintained and insured. They will also need to research and comply with any local regulations and permits required for renting out boats and RVs.

If you are considering renting out your boat or other recreational vehicle, there are several things you should consider ensuring you have a positive experience:

1. *Insurance*: Make sure you have adequate insurance coverage for your boat or recreational vehicle. Consider purchasing additional liability coverage for rental activities.
2. *Maintenance and repairs*: Keep your boat or recreational vehicle well-maintained to ensure it is safe and reliable for renters. Be prepared for the possibility of repairs or unexpected issues that may arise.

3. *Legal requirements*: Check with your state and local authorities to determine if you need any permits or licenses to legally rent out your boat or recreational vehicle.
4. *Rental agreements*: Develop a rental agreement that clearly outlines expectations, responsibilities, and liability for both you and the renter.
5. *Pricing:* Research the market to determine a fair price for your rental. Consider peak season rates, special promotions, and other factors that may impact pricing.
6. *Marketing*: Use online platforms, social media, and other marketing strategies to promote your rental and attract potential renters.
7. *Screening renters*: Develop a screening process to ensure you rent to responsible and trustworthy renters. Consider requiring a security deposit and verifying renters' identification and driving records.
8. *Safety equipment*: Ensure your boat or recreational vehicle is equipped with all necessary safety equipment, including life jackets, fire extinguishers, and first aid kits.

There are several platforms and websites that owners can use to rent out their boats and RVs, including *Boatsetter*, *GetMyBoat*, *Outdoorsy*, and *RVshare*. These platforms provide a secure way for owners to list their equipment, set rental prices, and communicate with renters. Owners can also choose to market their equipment through social media and other online channels to attract potential renters. Here are some additional resources to consider:

1. *Turo*: A car-sharing marketplace that allows car owners to rent out their vehicles to others.
2. *Camptoo*: A platform that connects private RV and campervan owners with renters in Europe.
3. *Boatbound*: A boat rental platform that offers insurance coverage for both boat owners and renters.
4. *Click*&Boat: A boat rental platform that operates in over 50 countries worldwide.

5. **RVnGO**: A platform for renting RVs and motorhomes, offering features like roadside assistance and 24/7 customer support.
6. **Sailo**: A boat rental marketplace that connects boat owners with renters and offers insurance coverage.

According to data from platforms such as **Boatsetter**, **GetMyBoat**, and **Outdoorsy**, boat owners can earn anywhere from a few hundred dollars to several thousand dollars per month by renting out their boats or recreational vehicles. For example, on **Boatsetter**, boat owners can earn an average of $4,500 per year by renting out their boats for just a few days each month.

According to data from platforms such as Outdoorsy and RVshare, RV owners can earn anywhere from a few hundred dollars to several thousand dollars per month by renting out their recreational vehicles. For example, on **Outdoorsy**, RV owners can earn an average of $36,000 per year by renting out their RVs for a few weeks each year.

The earning potential for renting out boats or recreational vehicles can be even higher in areas with high demand for such rentals, such as popular vacation destinations or areas with limited rental options. However, it's important to note that there may be additional expenses associated with renting out these types of vehicles, such as maintenance and insurance costs.

In general, renting out boats and RVs can be a lucrative and rewarding way to generate passive income while sharing the joy of outdoor recreation with others.

Rent Out Camping Spaces or Land for Events

Renting out camping spaces or land for events can be an excellent way to generate passive income. Landowners can use their property to host various events such as weddings, music festivals, and other outdoor activities. They can also rent out camping spaces for people who want to enjoy nature and explore the area.

Renting out camping spaces or land for events can be done in various ways, including partnering with event organizers or listing the space on websites that specialize in outdoor rentals. Landowners can earn a passive income by charging a fee for the use of the land or space.

To start renting out camping spaces or land for events, landowners need to consider the following factors:

1. *Location*: The location of the property plays a significant role in determining the demand for camping or event space.
2. *Facilities*: The facilities available on the property, such as electricity, water, restrooms, and showers, can also affect the rental price.
3. *Zoning and Permits*: Landowners need to check the zoning laws and obtain the necessary permits from the local authorities to rent out the property for events or camping.
4. *Liability*: Landowners should also consider the liability issues and obtain insurance coverage to protect themselves from any potential claims.
5. *Marketing*: To attract renters, landowners should market their space through social media, websites, and other outdoor rental platforms.

When advertising your camping spaces or land for events, be sure to include plenty of photos and a detailed description of your property. It's also important to be clear about any rules or restrictions, such as noise levels or maximum occupancy. There are several platforms you can use to advertise your camping spaces or land for events:

1. *Hipcamp*: This is a popular platform that connects landowners with people looking for unique camping experiences. You can list your land on Hipcamp and set your own rules and prices.
2. *Tentrr*: This platform allows you to offer fully equipped campsites on your land. Tentrr provides everything from the tent to the cooking equipment, and you get to keep 80% of the revenue.
3. *Campspace*: Similar to Hipcamp, Campspace connects landowners with people looking for unique camping experiences. You can list your land on Campspace and set your own rules and prices.
4. *EventUp*: This platform allows you to list your land as a venue for events such as weddings, parties, and corporate retreats. You can set your own prices and availability.
5. *Peerspace*: Similar to EventUp, Peerspace allows you to list your land as a venue for events. Peerspace also provides a concierge service to help with logistics and planning.

A great campsite should offer a beautiful and safe environment, accessible and well-maintained facilities, privacy, and proximity to natural features and wildlife. Additional qualities include:

1. *Location*: A great campsite should be in a scenic and peaceful environment, away from the noise and chaos of the city.
1. *Safety*: The campsite should be safe and secure, with amenities such as lighting, fire pits, and emergency services nearby.
2. *Accessibility*: The campsite should be easily accessible by car or on foot, with clear signage and a well-maintained entrance.
3. *Level ground*: The campsite should have a level and flat ground for setting up tents, camping equipment, and activities.
4. *Natural features*: A great campsite should have access to natural features such as rivers, lakes, mountains, and hiking trails.
5. *Cleanliness*: The campsite should be well-maintained and clean, with garbage and recycling facilities available.

6. *Privacy*: The campsite should offer some level of privacy from neighboring campsites, with enough distance between them to avoid feeling crowded.
7. *Amenities*: The campsite should have basic amenities such as clean water, toilets, and showers, as well as picnic tables and fire rings for cooking and gathering around.
8. *Wildlife*: A great campsite should offer the opportunity to observe wildlife in their natural habitat, without being intrusive or harmful to them.
9. *Weather protection*: The campsite should have natural or man-made features such as trees, bushes, or shelters to protect campers from extreme weather conditions.

The average income from renting out land for camping spaces can vary greatly depending on factors such as location, amenities, and demand. In some areas, it may be possible to charge several hundred dollars per night for a prime camping spot during peak season, while in less popular areas, the rate may be much lower.

Renting out camping spaces or land for events can be an excellent passive income idea for people who own land in attractive locations. It provides an opportunity to earn money while enjoying the outdoors and sharing their property with others.

Rent Out Your Land for Farming or Agriculture

Renting out your land for farming or agriculture can generate passive income by allowing farmers or agricultural businesses to use your land for crop cultivation or livestock grazing in exchange for rent payments. This can be a viable option for landowners who have unused or underutilized land that can be leased out to generate extra income.

To get started with renting out your land for farming or agriculture, you can first research and identify potential tenants in your area. You can reach out to local farming associations, agricultural cooperatives, or farm-to-market organizations to find interested farmers or businesses. Alternatively, you can also advertise your land on online platforms such as *FarmlandFinder* or *LandAndFarm*, which connect landowners with potential tenants.

Before renting out your land, you should also consider important factors such as the type of crops or livestock that will be raised, the duration of the lease agreement, and any legal requirements or permits that may be necessary. It is important to have a written lease agreement that outlines all the terms and conditions of the arrangement, including the rent amount, payment schedule, and responsibilities of both the tenant and the landowner.

Here are some additional resources for you to explore:

1. *FarmLink* - FarmLink is a platform that connects farmers with landowners. You can list your land on the platform and connect with farmers who are looking for land to rent.
2. *Local Farm Organizations* - Check with your local farm organizations to see if they have any programs or resources available for connecting landowners with farmers.
3. *Government Programs* - The *U.S. Department of Agriculture* has programs available to help connect landowners with farmers. Check their website or visit your local USDA office to learn more.

4. *Craigslist* or *Facebook Marketplace* - You can also list your land for rent on popular online marketplaces like Craigslist or Facebook Marketplace. Be sure to include detailed information about the size, location, and any restrictions or requirements you may have.

5. *Local Farmer's Markets* - If there are farmer's markets in your area, consider setting up a booth and advertising your land for rent. This can be a great way to connect with local farmers and find potential renters.

6. *Word of Mouth* - Spread the word to your friends, family, and neighbors that you have land available for rent. You never know who may be looking for land to farm or use for agriculture.

If you're considering renting out your land for farming or agriculture for passive income, here are some things to be aware of:

1. *Land quality*: The quality and type of land you own will determine what types of crops can be grown and the potential rental income.

2. *Soil testing*: Have the soil tested to determine if it's suitable for growing crops and if any necessary amendments are needed.

3. *Zoning and regulations*: Check zoning and regulations in your area to ensure that your land can be used for farming or agriculture and what permits or licenses are required.

4. *Lease agreements*: Draft a lease agreement that outlines the terms of the rental agreement, including rent, payment schedules, and responsibilities of both the landlord and tenant.

5. *Tenant selection*: Choose a tenant who has experience in farming and agriculture and who can maintain the land and crops.

6. *Insurance*: Consider liability insurance to protect yourself against any accidents or damages that may occur on the property.

7. *Tax implications*: Consult with a tax professional to understand the tax implications of rental income from farmland.

8. *Water supply*: Ensure that there is a reliable water supply for irrigation and farming.

9. *Maintenance and repairs*: Determine who will be responsible for maintaining and repairing any equipment or structures on the property.

10. ***Long-term planning***: Consider the long-term impacts of farming on the land and plan accordingly to maintain its fertility and value over time.

The average income from renting out land for farming or agriculture per month can vary greatly depending on factors such as location, soil quality, climate, and the type of crops or livestock being raised. The average cropland rental rate in the United States was $136 per acre per year, while the average pastureland rental rate was $12.50 per acre per year.

Assuming an acre of land is rented out for the full year, this would work out to be approximately $11.33 per acre per month for cropland and $1.04 per acre per month for pastureland. However, these figures can vary significantly depending on the region and type of agriculture being practiced. In some areas, such as prime farmland in California, rental rates may be much higher, while in less productive areas, rental rates may be lower. It is also worth noting that landowners who lease their land for agriculture may be eligible for various tax breaks and other incentives.

Remember to do your due diligence and thoroughly vet potential renters before signing any agreements. It's also a good idea to consult with a lawyer to ensure your rental agreement is legally binding and protects your interests as a landowner. Renting out your land for farming or agriculture can be a great way to generate passive income while also supporting local farmers and contributing to sustainable agriculture practices.

Rent Out Your Land for Solar Panel or Wind Turbines Installations

Renting out your land for solar panel or wind turbine installations can be a great way to generate passive income. This involves leasing a portion of your land to a company that will install solar panels or wind turbines to generate renewable energy.

The process involves finding a reputable company that specializes in renewable energy and negotiating a lease agreement. The company will typically conduct a site survey to determine if your land is suitable for the installation of solar panels or wind turbines.

Once the lease agreement is in place, the company will install the renewable energy system and maintain it over the duration of the lease. You will receive regular rental payments as compensation for the use of your land.

Renting out your land for solar panel or wind turbine installations can provide several benefits, including:

1. Passive income: You can earn regular rental payments without having to do any additional work.
2. Sustainable energy: By leasing your land for renewable energy installations, you are contributing to a more sustainable future.
3. Long-term income: Lease agreements can last for decades, providing a long-term source of income.
4. Reduced energy costs: In some cases, you may be able to negotiate reduced energy costs as part of the lease agreement.

Seps for renting out your land for solar panel or wind turbine installations should include contacting local renewable energy companies, researching lease agreements and legal requirements, and consulting with a professional to help negotiate the terms of the lease. Here are a few resources to assist with your research:

1. **Landmark Dividend**: A company that helps landowners monetize their land by leasing it for renewable energy projects, including solar and wind.
2. **Solar Land Partners**: A company that connects landowners with solar developers and helps negotiate lease agreements.
3. **Windustry**: A nonprofit organization that provides information and resources for landowners interested in leasing their land for wind energy projects.
4. **Renewable Properties**: A company that develops, finances, and operates solar energy projects on land leased from property owners.
5. **American Wind Energy Association**: A trade association that represents the wind energy industry and provides information on leasing land for wind turbines.
6. **Farmland LP**: A company that leases farmland for sustainable agriculture and renewable energy projects, including solar and wind.
7. **Solar Site Design**: A platform that connects landowners with solar developers and offers a streamlined process for leasing land for solar installations.
8. **SunShare**: A company that offers community solar programs, allowing landowners to lease their land for solar energy projects that benefit their local community.
9. **National Renewable Energy Laboratory**: A government research laboratory that provides resources and information on renewable energy projects, including solar and wind.
10. **The Solar Foundation**: A nonprofit organization that advocates for solar energy and provides resources for landowners interested in leasing their land for solar installations.

The amount of money you can expect to rent your land for solar panel or wind turbine installations can vary widely depending on several factors such as the location, size of the land, the potential for energy production, and the terms of the lease agreement.

On average, landowners can earn between $500 to $2,000 per acre per year for leasing their land for solar panel installations, while wind turbine installations can fetch higher rates of $3,000 to $8,000 per turbine per year. However, these rates can vary depending on the specific circumstances of your land and the energy project.

It's important to note that the amount of money you can earn from renting your land for renewable energy projects can also depend on the type of lease agreement you enter into. Some agreements may offer a fixed annual rate, while others may include a revenue-sharing arrangement that allows you to earn a percentage of the energy produced.

It's important to do your own research and due diligence before entering into any agreements with these or other companies. It's also a good idea to consult with a lawyer or financial advisor to ensure that you fully understand the legal and financial implications of renting out your land for renewable energy installations.

Rent Out Your Backyard for Events or Weddings

Renting out your backyard for weddings or events can be a great way to generate passive income. With the rise of outdoor weddings and events, many people are looking for unique and intimate spaces to host their special occasions. If you have a well-maintained backyard or garden, it could be the perfect venue for these events.

To get started, you'll need to make sure your backyard is suitable for events. This may include landscaping, adding seating areas, and ensuring there is enough space for guests. You'll also need to consider any noise restrictions or permits that may be required in your area.

Once you've prepared your backyard, you can start advertising your space for rent on wedding and event rental websites, local classifieds, and social media platforms. It's important to have clear policies in place regarding things like hours of use, maximum number of guests, and cleanup responsibilities. You may also want to consider hiring a property management company to handle bookings and logistics. Additional resources for you to consider include:

1. *PeerSpace*: PeerSpace is an online platform that allows property owners to rent out their spaces for events, photoshoots, meetings, and more. You can list your backyard as a unique venue on PeerSpace and attract potential renters.
2. *EventUp*: EventUp is another platform that connects property owners with event organizers. You can list your backyard as a potential venue on EventUp and set your own rates.
3. *Splacer*: Splacer is a platform that helps you monetize your space by renting it out for all sorts of events. You can use Splacer to list your backyard as a venue and reach a wider audience.
4. *Airbnb*: While Airbnb is primarily known for short-term vacation rentals, you can also list your backyard as a unique venue on the platform. This can be a great way to attract renters who are looking for a one-of-a-kind space for their event.

5. *Facebook Marketplace*: You can also list your backyard for rent on Facebook Marketplace. This can be a great option if you want to attract local renters who are looking for a unique venue for their event.

6. *Craigslist*: Finally, you can also list your backyard for rent on Craigslist. This can be a great way to reach potential renters in your local area who are looking for a unique space for their event.

The amount of money you can expect to make per month for renting your backyard out for events can vary widely depending on several factors such as the location, size of the backyard, the type and frequency of events, and the amenities offered. On average, property owners can charge between $50 to $500 per hour for renting out their backyard for events, depending on the type of event and the amenities provided. For example, a simple birthday party might rent for $50 to $150 per hour, while a wedding or larger event with access to amenities such as outdoor kitchens or restrooms can command higher rates, up to $500 per hour or more.

It's important to note that the demand for event rentals can vary depending on the season and location, and some months may be more profitable than others. Additionally, it's important to factor in any additional costs such as insurance or permits that may be required for hosting events on your property.

Remember to always do your due diligence when renting out your backyard for events. Make sure you have the proper permits and insurance and be clear about your expectations and rules for renters. Renting out your backyard for weddings and events can be a lucrative source of passive income, particularly during the summer months. With a little bit of preparation and marketing, you can turn your backyard into a popular event venue that generates income while requiring minimal effort on your part.

Rent Out Unused Space for Vending Machines

Renting out unused space for vending machines can be a profitable passive income idea. The basic concept involves leasing a space to a vending machine operator who will place and maintain their vending machines on the premises. The owner of the space earns a percentage of the revenue generated by the vending machines. This type of arrangement is beneficial for both parties as the vending machine operator gains access to a profitable location while the owner earns income from an unused space.

There are several advantages to renting out unused space for vending machines. Firstly, it requires minimal effort from the owner as the vending machine operator is responsible for maintenance, restocking, and collecting money from the machines. Secondly, vending machines can be placed in a variety of locations, including office buildings, hospitals, schools, and shopping centers, providing a wide range of options for owners looking to rent out their space. Finally, the income generated from vending machines can be relatively stable, as people will always need snacks and beverages, making it a reliable source of passive income.

To get started, owners can contact vending machine operators directly or use third-party companies that connect owners with vending machine operators. It's important to do research on the vending machine operator and negotiate a fair contract that outlines the percentage of revenue the owner will receive and the responsibilities of both parties. Additionally, owners should ensure that the location of the vending machines is safe and accessible to customers.

Some of the largest vending machine companies that offer rental opportunities for unused space include:

1. *Coca-Cola*: The Coca-Cola Company offers vending machines for rent and has a wide variety of beverage options available.

2. *PepsiCo*: PepsiCo operates a vending machine division called PepsiCo Beverages and Foods North America, which provides vending machines and product options for rental.
3. *SnackMate*: SnackMate is a vending machine company that offers snacks, beverages, and other products for rent in various locations.
4. *7-Eleven*: 7-Eleven is a convenience store chain that also operates vending machines in various locations. They offer rental opportunities for unused space in high-traffic areas.
5. *Canteen Vending Services*: Canteen Vending Services is one of the largest vending machine companies in the world, providing vending machines and services to various industries.
6. *Aramark*: Aramark is a multinational company that provides vending machines and food services to businesses, schools, and other organizations.
7. *Vending Solutions*: Vending Solutions is a vending machine company that offers various types of machines and product options for rental.

Renting unused land for vending machines can be a potentially profitable way to generate passive income, but there are several things you should be aware of before starting:

1. *Location*: The location of your vending machine can impact its profitability. You need to find a high-traffic area with potential customers and make sure the land you rent is zoned for vending machines.
2. *Vending Machine Type*: The type of vending machine you choose can impact its profitability and customer appeal. You need to select vending machines that offer products that are in demand and priced competitively.
3. *Product Inventory*: You need to keep your vending machine stocked with inventory to ensure it remains profitable. You need to have a system in place for purchasing and stocking inventory, as well as monitoring sales and adjusting inventory levels as needed.
4. *Maintenance and Repair*: Vending machines require regular maintenance and repair to ensure they remain in good working

order. You need to have a system in place for cleaning, restocking, and repairing your vending machines.

5. ***Contract and Lease Terms***: You need to have a written contract and lease agreement in place that outlines the terms of your rental agreement. You should consider factors such as rent, lease duration, payment terms, and renewal options.

6. ***Legal Issues***: Renting land for vending machines is subject to regulations and legal issues, such as liability insurance, taxes, and permits. It's important to comply with all regulations and consult with legal and financial professionals as needed.

The amount of money you can expect to make per month for renting unused space to vending machine companies can vary widely depending on several factors such as the location, foot traffic, type of vending machines, and the terms of the lease agreement.

On average, property owners can expect to receive around $50 to $100 per month per vending machine, although this can vary depending on the demand for the products and the commission rate offered by the vending machine company.

For example, if you have three vending machines on your property, you could potentially earn around $150 to $300 per month in passive income. However, it's important to note that this amount can be higher or lower depending on the specific circumstances of your property and the vending machines.

Renting unused space to vending machine companies can be a lucrative way to generate passive income without much effort. By partnering with a reputable vending machine company, property owners can earn regular rent payments and potentially increase foot traffic to their property. However, it is important to carefully review the terms of the lease agreement and ensure that the vending machines are maintained and serviced regularly to avoid any liability issues. Overall, renting unused space to vending machine companies is a great way to generate passive income while making efficient use of underutilized space.

Rent Out Billboard Space

Renting out billboard space is an effective way to generate passive income. It involves leasing space on a billboard to companies or advertisers who want to display their advertisements. Billboards are typically located in high traffic areas, making them an attractive advertising option for businesses.

To get started with renting out billboard space, you will need to find a suitable location for a billboard. Ideally, the location should be visible to many people, such as along a busy highway or in a city center. Once you have identified a suitable location, you can contact outdoor advertising companies that specialize in billboard advertising to lease the space. These companies will take care of the installation, maintenance, and removal of the billboard, and will pay you a monthly fee for the use of your property.

The amount of money you can earn from renting out billboard space will depend on several factors, such as the size and location of the billboard, the traffic volume in the area, and the demand for advertising space in the market. In general, the larger and more visible the billboard, the higher the rental fee you can command. Some of the largest billboard companies that rent out spaces for advertising include:

1. *Lamar Advertising* - Lamar is one of the largest outdoor advertising companies in North America, with more than 348,000 displays across the United States, Canada, and Puerto Rico.
2. *Clear Channel Outdoor* - Clear Channel Outdoor operates in over 30 countries and is one of the largest outdoor advertising companies in the world. They offer a wide variety of outdoor advertising solutions, including billboards, digital displays, and transit advertising.
3. *Outfront Media* - Outfront Media is a leading outdoor advertising company in North America, with more than 500,000 displays across the United States and Canada. They offer a variety of outdoor advertising solutions, including billboards, transit advertising, and digital displays.

4. ***JCDecaux*** - JCDecaux is a global outdoor advertising company with more than 1 million displays in over 80 countries. They offer a variety of outdoor advertising solutions, including billboards, street furniture, and transit advertising.
5. ***Adams Outdoor Advertising*** - Adams Outdoor Advertising is a privately-owned company that operates in 10 states across the United States. They offer a variety of outdoor advertising solutions, including billboards, digital displays, and transit advertising.

It's important to note that each company may have different requirements for renting out billboard space, such as location, size, and visibility. It's best to contact the companies directly to inquire about renting out your space for advertising. The average income from renting out billboard space per month can vary widely depending on factors such as location, size of the billboard, and the amount of traffic passing by.

Rental rates are typically quoted in terms of cost per "impression," which refers to the number of times that someone sees the advertisement on the billboard. According to industry estimates, the average cost per impression from $2 to $8. Based on this estimate, if a billboard generates 50,000 impressions per month, the rental income could range from $100 to $400 per month. Be aware that these are just estimates and the actual rental income can vary significantly depending on the specific circumstances of the billboard location and the rental agreement.

Renting out billboard space can be a great way to generate passive income, as you will receive a monthly payment for the duration of the lease without having to do any ongoing work or maintenance. However, it's important to do your due diligence and ensure that you are working with reputable outdoor advertising companies to avoid any potential issues or legal disputes.

Rent Out Signage Space

Renting out signage space refers to allowing other businesses or individuals to place their signs on your property, such as the exterior of your building or a fence facing a busy road. This can be an effective way to generate passive income, as you are essentially earning money for doing nothing more than allowing someone to use your space.

One of the main benefits of renting out signage space is that it can provide a steady stream of income. The amount you can earn will depend on factors such as the location of your property, the size and visibility of the signage space, and the demand for advertising in your area.

To get started with renting out signage space, you will need to identify potential renters. This could include local businesses, advertising agencies, or even individuals looking to promote a personal cause or event. You can advertise your signage space for rent through local classifieds, social media, or by reaching out to businesses and organizations directly.

It is important to have a clear agreement in place with your renters, outlining the terms of the rental, including the length of the rental, the cost, and any restrictions on the type of signage that can be displayed. It is also a good idea to have liability insurance to protect yourself in case of any accidents or damage to the signage.

There are several types of organizations that rent signage space from people. Here are some examples:

1. *Small Businesses*: Local small businesses often rent signage space from property owners in their area. They may be looking to advertise their products or services to people passing by.
2. *Non-profit Organizations*: Non-profit organizations often use signage to promote their events, fundraisers, or causes. They may rent signage space from property owners to help spread the word.
3. *Event Companies*: Event companies may rent signage space to promote upcoming events, concerts, or festivals. They often look for high-traffic areas to attract more attendees.

4. ***Political Campaigns***: Political campaigns may rent signage space to promote their candidates or issues during election season. They may be looking for visible locations near polling places or busy intersections.

5. ***Advertising Agencies***: Advertising agencies may rent signage space on behalf of their clients. They often look for strategic locations with high visibility and foot traffic.

It's important to note that laws and regulations regarding signage vary by location. Before renting out signage space, it's important to research local regulations and obtain any necessary permits or licenses. Renting out signage space can be a relatively simple way to generate passive income, if you have the space available and are willing to do a bit of marketing and negotiation to find renters.

Rent Out Your Shed Space

Renting out shed space is a great way to generate passive income. You can rent out your shed to individuals, businesses, or organizations that need extra storage space for their belongings, equipment, or inventory. This can be an excellent option if you have an unused shed on your property that you don't use very often.

To start renting out your shed space, you'll need to make sure that it's in good condition and that it's secure. You should also make sure that you have enough space to accommodate the needs of potential renters.

One of the advantages of renting out shed space is that you can charge a monthly rent for the space, which can generate passive income. You can also set a lease term, so you know exactly how long the space will be rented out for.

Additionally, you may want to consider offering additional services such as electricity, water, and access to bathroom facilities to increase the appeal of your rental. This can help you attract more potential renters and generate more income.

There are several online platforms that you can use to advertise your shed space rental, including websites like *Craigslist*, *Facebook Marketplace*, and storage rental websites. Make sure to provide clear and detailed information about the size and condition of the shed, as well as any additional amenities or services that you're offering.

There are a variety of free resources available online that can help you create rental contracts for your shed space. Here are a few options:

1. *Legal Templates*: This website offers a variety of free rental agreement templates, including ones for storage sheds. You can customize the template to include all the details you need for your specific rental situation.
2. *Rocket Lawyer*: This website offers a free customizable storage lease agreement template that you can use to create a rental contract for your shed space.

3. *LawDepot*: This website offers a variety of free legal documents, including a storage space rental agreement. You can customize the template to include your own terms and conditions.
4. *PandaDoc*: This website offers a free storage rental agreement template that you can use to create a rental contract for your shed space. The template is customizable and can be downloaded in a variety of formats.
5. *HelloSign*: This website offers a free, customizable storage rental agreement template that you can use to create a rental contract for your shed space. You can add your own terms and conditions, and the template is available in a variety of formats for easy sharing and signing.

It's important to note that these resources can provide a starting point, but it's always a good idea to consult with a lawyer to ensure that your rental contract is legally binding and covers all the necessary details for your specific rental situation.

Renting out your shed for passive income can be a potentially profitable venture, but there are several things you should be aware of before starting:

1. *Shed Condition*: The condition of your shed can impact its profitability and customer appeal. You need to make sure the shed is structurally sound, clean, and in good condition before renting it out.
2. *Zoning and Permits*: You need to check local zoning laws and permits to ensure that you are allowed to rent out your shed for residential or commercial purposes. You should also consider obtaining liability insurance to protect yourself in case of accidents or damages.
3. *Tenant Screening*: You need to screen potential tenants carefully to ensure that they are reliable, responsible, and will take good care of your property. This can include running background checks and checking references.
4. *Maintenance and Repairs*: You need to have a system in place for maintaining and repairing your shed. This can include regular inspections, cleaning, and repairs as needed.

5. *Utilities and Services*: You need to consider whether you will provide utilities and services, such as electricity and water, to your tenant. If so, you should include this in the rental agreement and make sure that the tenant is responsible for any associated costs.

The amount of money you can make by renting out signage space can vary greatly depending on a variety of factors such as location, size, visibility, and demand. For example, if your signage is located in a high-traffic area with high visibility and demand, you can potentially earn several thousand dollars per month. On the other hand, if your signage is located in a less busy area or has limited visibility, you may only be able to generate a few hundred dollars per month.

It's difficult to give an exact figure for the average amount of money earned from renting out signage space per month since it depends on so many variables. However, according to some industry estimates, you could expect to earn anywhere from $100 to $10,000 per month or more, depending on the size and location of your signage.

Overall, renting out shed space can be a great way to generate passive income, especially if you have an unused shed on your property. With the right preparation and advertising, you can attract renters and start earning money right away.

Rent Out Your Attic Space

Renting out attic space can be a great way to generate passive income, especially if you have unused space in your home. Attic space can be used for storage, or even as a living space if it is finished and has the necessary amenities.

To start renting out your attic space, you'll need to make sure it is safe and accessible. You'll want to ensure that it meets all building codes and safety regulations, and that there is a safe way to access it, such as a sturdy ladder or staircase. You'll also want to make sure that the attic is clean and free of any hazards, such as mold or pests.

Once your attic is ready, you can start advertising it for rent. You can use online marketplaces such as Craigslist, Airbnb, or HomeAway to list your space and find potential renters. You can also reach out to local storage facilities or real estate agencies to see if they have any clients who are looking for additional storage space or living space.

When renting out your attic space, it's important to have a written agreement with your tenants that outlines the terms of the rental, such as the rental period, rental price, and any restrictions or rules for using the space. You may also want to require renters to carry renters' insurance to protect your property in case of damage or theft.

Before renting out your attic space for storage, there are a few tips you should keep in mind for storing things safely:

1. *Declutter*: Before you start storing items in your attic, make sure you declutter the space. Get rid of anything you no longer need or want and organize the remaining items. This will make it easier to keep the space tidy and prevent damage to stored items.
2. *Use protective covers*: When storing items, use protective covers to prevent damage from dust, moisture, and insects. This is particularly important if you're storing items for a long time.
3. *Install proper ventilation*: Attics can get hot and stuffy, which can damage stored items. Make sure your attic has proper ventilation, such as vents or fans, to keep air circulating and prevent damage.

4. *Consider weight* limits: Attics are not designed to hold a lot of weight, so be mindful of the weight of items you store in the space. This is particularly important if you're storing heavy items, such as furniture or appliances.

5. *Keep* a *clear path*: Make sure there is a clear path in your attic so renters can safely access their stored items. This will also make it easier for you to check on the space periodically and ensure everything is in order.

6. *Use sturdy shelving*: If you're storing a lot of items, consider installing sturdy shelving to help organize the space and make it easier for renters to access their items. Make sure the shelving is properly secured and can support the weight of the stored items.

7. *Inspect regularly*: Make sure to inspect the attic regularly for any signs of damage or problems, such as leaks or pests. Address any issues promptly to prevent damage to stored items and maintain a safe and secure storage space for renters.

Renting out your attic for passive income can be a potentially profitable venture, but there are several things you should be aware of before starting:

1. *Attic Condition*: The condition of your attic can impact its profitability and customer appeal. You need to make sure the attic is structurally sound, clean, and in good condition before renting it out.

2. *Zoning and Permits*: You need to check local zoning laws and permits to ensure that you are allowed to rent out your attic for residential or commercial purposes. You should also consider obtaining liability insurance to protect yourself in case of accidents or damages.

3. *Safety and Accessibility*: You need to ensure that your attic is safe and accessible for tenants. This can include installing a secure staircase or ladder, providing adequate lighting, and ensuring that the space meets building code requirements.

4. *Rental Agreement*: You need to have a written rental agreement in place that outlines the terms of your rental agreement. This

should include details such as rent, lease duration, payment terms, and expectations for the tenant.

5. *Tenant Screening*: You need to screen potential tenants carefully to ensure that they are reliable, responsible, and will take good care of your property. This can include running background checks and checking references.

6. *Maintenance and Repairs*: You need to have a system in place for maintaining and repairing your attic. This can include regular inspections, cleaning, and repairs as needed.

7. *Utilities and Services*: You need to consider whether you will provide utilities and services, such as electricity and water, to your tenant. If so, you should include this in the rental agreement and make sure that the tenant is responsible for any associated costs.

The amount an individual can make renting out attic space per month can vary greatly depending on factors such as location, size of the attic, and demand for storage space in the area.

In some areas, attic space may not be in high demand and may only fetch a few hundred dollars per month. However, in areas with high demand for storage space, attic rentals can range from $50 to $200 per month or more for a small to medium-sized space.

It's important to note that there may be additional costs associated with renting out attic space, such as insurance and safety requirements, that can impact the overall profitability of this passive income stream.

Renting out attic space can be a great way to generate passive income from your home, if you take the necessary steps to ensure it is safe, accessible, and properly advertised. With the right preparation and advertising, you can attract renters and start earning money immediately.

Rent Out Your Time

Renting out your time is not a typical form of passive income as it involves actively exchanging your time for money. However, it can still be a way to generate income in a flexible and potentially lucrative way. Here are a few examples:

1. *Freelancing*: If you have a particular skill or expertise, such as writing, graphic design, programming, or social media management, you can offer your services on freelance marketplaces like *Upwork*, *Fiverr*, or *Freelancer*. You can set your own rates and work with clients on a project-by-project basis, allowing you to work from anywhere and choose your own hours.

2. *Coaching or consulting*: If you have expertise in a particular area, such as business, health and wellness, or personal development, you can offer coaching or consulting services to clients. You can do this through one-on-one sessions or group coaching, and you can work with clients in person or online.

3. *Teaching or tutoring*: If you have knowledge in a particular subject area, you can offer your services as a teacher or tutor. This can include tutoring in academic subjects, teaching music or art lessons, or offering workshops or classes on a particular skill or topic.

4. *Virtual assistance*: Many businesses and individuals need help with administrative tasks, such as email management, scheduling, and data entry. You can offer your services as a virtual assistant and work with clients remotely, allowing you to work from anywhere and choose your own hours.

To get started with renting out your time, you can create a profile on freelance marketplaces, advertise your services on social media or online classifieds, or reach out to potential clients directly. It's important to set clear rates and expectations upfront, and to have a contract or agreement in place to protect both you and your clients.

There are many freelance marketplaces available where you can rent out your time and skills. Some of the most popular ones include:

1. *Upwork*: Upwork is one of the largest and most well-known freelance marketplaces. It offers a wide variety of job categories and allows freelancers to set their own rates.
2. *Fiverr*: Fiverr is a popular platform that allows freelancers to offer their services at a fixed price. It is known for its affordability and offers a wide range of job categories.
3. *Freelancer*: Freelancer is a global marketplace that offers a range of job categories, including programming, writing, design, and more.
4. *PeoplePerHour*: PeoplePerHour is a UK-based marketplace that offers a range of freelance services, including writing, design, programming, and more.
5. *Guru*: Guru is a global marketplace that offers a wide range of job categories, including programming, design, writing, and more.
6. *Toptal*: Toptal is a platform that connects businesses with top-tier freelance talent in fields such as software development, design, and finance.
7. *99designs*: 99designs is a platform specifically for design work, including logo design, web design, and more.
8. *TaskRabbit*: TaskRabbit is a platform that connects people with local freelance labor for tasks such as cleaning, moving, and handyman work.

If you're considering renting out your time for passive income, there are several things to be aware of. Here are some key considerations:

1. *Determine your availability*: It's important to determine how much time you're willing to commit to renting out your time. Make sure you have a clear understanding of your availability and schedule before committing to any rental agreements.
2. *Set clear boundaries*: Be sure to set clear boundaries with your renters, such as hours of availability, services offered, and expectations. This will help ensure that everyone is on the same page and prevent misunderstandings.
3. *Determine your rates*: Research the going rates for similar services in your area to determine what you should charge. You may need to adjust your rates based on demand and competition.

4. ***Consider liability issues***: Depending on the type of service you're offering, you may need to consider liability issues. Make sure you have the proper insurance coverage and understand your legal responsibilities.
5. ***Have a clear contract***: It's important to have a clear, written contract that outlines the terms of the rental agreement. This can help prevent misunderstandings and protect both you and your renters.
6. ***Be prepared for customer service***: Renting out your time means you're essentially running a small business. Be prepared to provide excellent customer service and handle any issues that arise in a professional manner.
7. ***Be aware of tax implications***: Rental income is generally taxable, so be sure to consult with a tax professional to understand the tax implications of renting out your time.

The income of a freelancer can vary greatly depending on their industry, skillset, experience, location, and other factors. According to a survey conducted by Upwork and Freelancers Union, the average freelancer earns around $31 per hour, which equates to an annual income of around $64,000 if they work full-time. However, it's important to note that many freelancers work part-time or have inconsistent workloads, which can impact their overall income. Additionally, some highly skilled freelancers, such as software developers or designers, may earn significantly more than the average.

These are just a few examples of freelance marketplaces where you can rent out your time and skills. Each platform has its own strengths and weaknesses, so it's important to do your research and find the one that's best for you.

Chapter 6: Social Media Opportunities

Instagram Influencer Marketing

Instagram influencer marketing is a rapidly growing industry that allows individuals to leverage their social media following to earn money through sponsored content. Influencers can promote products, services, and brands to their followers and earn a commission on any resulting sales or clicks.

To become an Instagram influencer, one must first establish a strong following and build a personal brand that aligns with the products or services they wish to promote. This requires consistency in posting content that is engaging and resonates with their audience.

Once an influencer has a strong following, they can begin partnering with brands for sponsored content. Brands will typically approach influencers who have a strong following in their target audience and who have a proven track record of engagement and sales conversions.

In addition to sponsored content, influencers can also earn money through affiliate marketing. This involves promoting products or services on behalf of a brand and earning a commission on any resulting sales.

To be successful in Instagram influencer marketing, it is important to remain authentic and transparent with followers. Influencers should only promote products or services they genuinely believe in and disclose any sponsored content to maintain trust with their audience.

Becoming an Instagram influencer takes time, effort, and strategy. Here are some resources to help you get started:

1. *Instagram*: Instagram is the primary platform for influencer marketing. Create an account, choose a niche or topic you're passionate about, and start building a following.
2. *Hashtags*: Use relevant hashtags to increase the visibility of your posts. Research popular hashtags in your niche and use them strategically to reach a broader audience.
3. *Content Creation*: Create high-quality content that resonates with your audience. Use a mix of photos, videos, and captions to engage your followers.

4. *Engagement*: Engage with your followers and other influencers in your niche. Respond to comments, participate in conversations, and build relationships with your followers.

5. *Analytics*: Use Instagram analytics to track your progress and optimize your strategy. Track metrics like follower growth, engagement rates, and the performance of each post to improve your content and grow your following.

6. *Influencer Networks*: Join influencer networks to find brand deals and collaborations. Networks like *AspireIQ*, *Tribe*, and *Influence.co* can connect you with brands looking for influencers in your niche.

7. *Courses* and *Workshops*: Invest in courses or workshops to learn more about influencer marketing. Platforms like *Udemy* and *Skillshare* offer courses on social media marketing and Instagram strategy.

The amount an Instagram influencer can make per month can vary greatly and depends on various factors such as the number of followers, engagement rate, niche, and brand partnerships. According to Influencer Marketing Hub, influencers with 50,000 to 100,000 followers can make an average of $500 to $1,000 per sponsored post, while those with over 1 million followers can make an average of $10,000 per post. However, these are just estimates and actual earnings can vary widely based on individual circumstances.

Remember, becoming an influencer takes time and patience. Stay consistent, stay engaged with your followers, and keep creating high-quality content that resonates with your audience. With dedication and hard work, anyone can become a successful Instagram influencer and earn passive income through sponsored content and affiliate marketing.

YouTube Ad Revenue

YouTube ad revenue can generate passive income by allowing creators to earn money from the advertisements that run on their videos. To start earning money from ad revenue, creators need to first apply to the YouTube Partner Program and meet the eligibility requirements, including having at least 1,000 subscribers and 4,000 watch hours in the past 12 months.

Once accepted into the program, creators can monetize their videos by enabling ads to run on them. YouTube pays a portion of the ad revenue to the creator, with the exact amount depending on factors such as the number of views, engagement, and the types of ads that appear on the video.

To increase the chances of earning more ad revenue, creators need to consistently upload high-quality content that attracts and retains viewers. They can also promote their videos on social media and other platforms to increase their audience and views.

There are several resources that can help you create quality content on YouTube:

1. *YouTube Creator Academy*: This is a free resource provided by YouTube itself. It provides various tutorials and courses to help creators improve their content creation skills.
2. *Video Editing Software*: There are many video editing software options available such as Adobe Premiere Pro, Final Cut Pro, iMovie, and DaVinci Resolve. These can help you edit your videos and make them more engaging.
3. *YouTube SEO Tools*: To optimize your video's performance, you can use various SEO tools such as *TubeBuddy*, *VidIQ,* and *Google Keyword Planner* to find the best keywords for your video titles, tags, and descriptions.
4. Microphone and Camera: High-quality audio and video are important for creating engaging content. You can invest in a good microphone and camera to enhance the quality of your content.

5. Music and Sound Effects: Using music and sound effects can add to the overall quality of your videos. Websites such as *AudioJungle* and *Epidemic Sound* provide royalty-free music and sound effects that you can use in your videos.
6. Stock Footage: If you need additional footage for your videos, you can use stock footage from websites such as *Shutterstock*, *Pexels*, and *Unsplash*. These sites provide free and paid footage that you can use to enhance your content.
7. Collaboration: Collaborating with other *YouTubers* can help you create better content and reach a wider audience. You can also share each other's audiences and benefit from each other's subscribers.

Becoming a top content creator on YouTube requires dedication and effort. Here are some tips that can help you:

1. *Consistency*: Consistency is key when it comes to creating content on YouTube. Your viewers will expect regular uploads, so try to stick to a schedule that works for you.
2. *Quality*: Quality is more important than quantity. Make sure your videos are well-produced and engaging, with good lighting, sound, and editing.
3. *SEO*: YouTube is the second-largest search engine in the world, so make sure your videos are optimized for search. Use relevant keywords in your titles, descriptions, and tags.
4. *Engagement*: Engage with your viewers by responding to comments and encouraging discussion. This will help build a community around your channel.
5. *Collaboration*: Collaborating with other YouTubers can help grow your audience and introduce you to new viewers.
6. *Creativity*: The ability to come up with new and unique ideas is essential for being a top content creator on YouTube. This means thinking outside the box and finding ways to stand out from the crowd.
7. *Authenticity*: Viewers can often tell when someone is being fake or inauthentic, so it's important for top content creators to be true to themselves and their brand. They don't try to be someone they're

not, and they aren't afraid to be vulnerable or share their personal experiences.

8. ***Engaging personality***: Top content creators on YouTube are often charismatic and engaging, making it easy for viewers to connect with them. They're relatable and make their audience feel like they're part of the conversation.

9. ***Strong work ethic***: Creating content for YouTube is hard work, and top content creators understand that. They're willing to put in the time and effort to make their videos the best they can be, and they don't give up easily.

10. ***Adaptability***: The YouTube platform is constantly evolving, so top content creators need to be able to adapt to changes and trends. They're not afraid to try new things and experiment with different types of content to see what works best for their audience.

11. ***Analyze and adjust***: Use YouTube analytics to track your performance and adjust your strategy accordingly. See which videos perform well and which ones don't and use that information to improve your content.

The amount of money earned through YouTube Ad Revenue varies greatly depending on a variety of factors such as the number of views, the type of content, the audience demographics, and the advertiser demand. Therefore, it is difficult to provide an accurate average amount as it can range from a few dollars to thousands of dollars per month.

According to a study by Influencer ***Marketing Hub*** in 2021, the average YouTuber can earn $3 to $5 per 1000 views from ads. This means that a video with 100,000 views could generate $300 to $500 in ad revenue. However, this is just an estimate and there are many factors that can affect this figure.

Remember, earning significant passive income from YouTube ad revenue requires a significant amount of effort and time invested in creating and promoting high-quality content that resonates with viewers. However, once established, it can provide a steady source of income with relatively little additional effort required.

YouTube Sponsorships

YouTube sponsorships are a popular way for content creators to generate passive income through their YouTube channels. A sponsorship is essentially a partnership between the creator and a brand or company, in which the creator promotes the brand's product or service in their videos.

Typically, a brand will reach out to a YouTuber whose content aligns with their target audience and offer a sponsorship deal. The specifics of the deal can vary, but usually involve the YouTuber promoting the brand in a specific video or series of videos in exchange for payment or compensation.

Sponsorships can be a great way for YouTubers to earn passive income, as they don't require ongoing effort or maintenance once the sponsored content is created and published. However, it's important for creators to be selective about the sponsorships they accept, ensuring that they align with their personal brand and values, and that they provide value to their audience.

Here are some resources for growing your YouTube following:

1. *YouTube Creator Academy*: This is an official resource provided by YouTube that offers courses and lessons on how to create and grow a successful YouTube channel.
2. *Social Blade*: This website provides information on the top YouTubers, their rankings, and their statistics. You can use this information to analyze the competition and find ways to improve your own content.
3. *VidIQ*: This is a tool that can help you optimize your videos for better performance on YouTube. It provides keyword research, analytics, and other useful features to help you grow your channel.
4. *TubeBuddy*: Similar to VidIQ, TubeBuddy is a tool that can help you optimize your videos for better performance on YouTube. It offers a variety of features including keyword research, analytics, and promotion tools.

5. *YouTube Partner Program*: Once you meet the requirements, you can join the YouTube Partner Program which allows you to monetize your videos and earn money from ads, memberships, and merchandise sales.

6. *Collaborations*: Collaborating with other YouTubers can help you reach a wider audience and gain new subscribers. Look for creators in your niche and reach out to them for collaboration opportunities.

7. *Social media promotion*: Promote your YouTube channel on social media platforms like Twitter, Instagram, and Facebook. This can help you reach a wider audience and gain new subscribers.

8. *Consistency*: Consistently uploading high-quality content is key to growing your YouTube channel. Set a schedule for your uploads and stick to it to keep your audience engaged and coming back for more.

Once you've grown your channel to a healthy audience, there are several resources you can then use to attract YouTube sponsorships:

1. *FameBit*: FameBit is an influencer marketing platform that connects YouTubers with brands looking for sponsorships. You can create a profile and browse through available sponsorship opportunities. The platform is free to use, and you get paid once the sponsorship is completed.

2. *Grapevine*: Grapevine is another influencer marketing platform that connects YouTubers with brands. You can apply for sponsorship opportunities directly on the platform, and once you are accepted, you can negotiate the terms and create content for the brand.

3. *YouTube Partner Program*: The YouTube Partner Program is a way for YouTubers to monetize their channels by displaying ads. Once you reach 1,000 subscribers and 4,000 watch hours, you can apply for the program. Once accepted, you can start earning money from ads displayed on your videos.

4. *Social Bluebook*: Social Bluebook is a platform that helps YouTubers determine their worth and negotiate deals with brands. You can create a profile on the platform, and it will calculate your

value based on your followers, engagement, and other metrics. You can then apply for sponsorships directly on the platform.

5. ***BrandSnob***: BrandSnob is a platform that connects YouTubers with brands looking for sponsorships. You can create a profile and browse through available sponsorship opportunities. The platform is free to use, and you get paid once the sponsorship is completed.

It is difficult to determine an average amount for YouTube sponsorships as it varies greatly depending on the individual creator's audience size, engagement, niche, and other factors. Generally, creators with larger and more engaged audiences can command higher sponsorship rates.

According to a survey by Influencer ***Marketing Hub***, the average rate for a sponsored video on YouTube in 2021 was $0.10 to $0.30 per view, meaning a video with 100,000 views could earn between $10,000 and $30,000. However, it is important to note that these are just estimates and many creators negotiate their own rates with brands.

It's also worth noting that not all YouTubers have sponsorship deals, and many rely solely on ad revenue or other forms of monetization. Additionally, some creators may choose to work with smaller or niche brands that may offer lower rates but are still valuable partnerships.

Remember, much like Instagram, growing your YouTube channel takes time and patience. Stay consistent, stay engaged with your followers, and keep creating high-quality content that resonates with your audience. With dedication and hard work, anyone can become a successful YouTube creator and earn passive income through sponsored content.

Facebook Ads

Facebook Ads can generate passive income by allowing individuals to earn money through advertising on their Facebook page. This process involves creating content that will attract an audience and then using Facebook Ads to promote that content. When a person clicks on the ad or interacts with it, the advertiser pays a fee to Facebook, and the individual who posted the content receives a portion of that fee.

To get started with Facebook Ads, individuals should first create a Facebook page or group focused on a particular niche or topic. This could be anything from a food blog to a fitness page. Once the page or group is created, individuals can start posting content and building their audience.

To monetize their page or group through Facebook Ads, individuals can sign up for *Facebook's Ad Breaks program*. This program allows creators to insert short ads into their videos and earn a percentage of the revenue generated by those ads.

Other ways to generate passive income through Facebook Ads include promoting affiliate products, creating sponsored posts, or selling products directly through Facebook Marketplace.

Here are some resources to get started with Facebook ads as a passive income stream:

1. *Facebook Ads Help Center*: This is Facebook's official resource for advertisers and includes information on creating and managing ads, targeting options, and best practices for success.
2. *Facebook Blueprint*: Facebook's training platform provides free courses on how to use Facebook Ads effectively, covering topics such as targeting, creative best practices, and ad optimization.
3. *Udemy*: Udemy offers a variety of courses on Facebook Ads, ranging from beginner to advanced level, that can help you learn how to create successful campaigns and drive more conversions.
4. *Social Media Examiner*: Social Media Examiner is a popular blog that covers social media marketing, including Facebook Ads. They

offer a range of articles and resources to help you learn more about Facebook Ads and how to use them effectively.

5. ***Facebook Ads Community***: Joining a Facebook Ads community, such as the Facebook Ad Buyers group, can be a great way to learn from other advertisers, share tips and tricks, and stay up to date on the latest trends and changes in the platform.

6. ***Outsource***: If you don't have the time or expertise to manage Facebook Ads campaigns yourself, consider outsourcing to a freelancer or agency that specializes in Facebook Ads management. This can be a great way to generate passive income by earning a percentage of the ad spend as commission.

If you're considering using Facebook Ads for passive income, here are some things to be aware of:

1. ***Facebook Ads require ongoing monitoring***: While Facebook Ads can be an effective way to generate passive income, they require ongoing monitoring and adjustments to optimize their performance. This means you'll need to spend time analyzing your ad metrics, adjusting your targeting and creative, and testing different strategies to ensure you're getting the best results.

2. ***Targeting is key***: With Facebook Ads, targeting is key to reaching the right audience and generating conversions. Make sure you take the time to research your target audience and use Facebook's targeting options to reach them effectively.

3. ***Ad creative matters***: Your ad creative (i.e. images or videos) can make or break the success of your Facebook Ads. Make sure your creative is eye-catching, relevant to your audience, and aligns with your messaging.

4. ***Budget wisely***: While Facebook Ads can be relatively inexpensive compared to traditional advertising methods, it's important to budget wisely to ensure you're getting a good return on investment. Set a budget that aligns with your goals and monitor your ad spend regularly to make sure you're staying within your budget.

5. ***Understand Facebook's policies***: Facebook has strict policies around advertising, including what types of content are allowed and how ads must be structured. Make sure you understand these

policies and comply with them to avoid having your ads rejected or your account suspended.

6. ***Test and optimize***: To maximize the effectiveness of your Facebook Ads, it's important to test different strategies and optimize your campaigns based on the results. This can include testing different ad formats, targeting options, and creative to see what works best for your audience.

The amount of money an average person can earn per month with Facebook Ads depends on several factors, such as the niche, target audience, ad budget, and ad placement. Generally, Facebook Ads can generate significant revenue for businesses and individuals who use it effectively to reach their target audience and promote their products or services.

According to a survey by ***Hootsuite***, the average cost per click (CPC) for Facebook Ads across all industries was $0.97 in 2020. However, this varies widely depending on the industry and the competition for ad space in that industry. The cost per click for ads in some industries can be much higher, while in others, it can be much lower.

Additionally, the amount of money earned through Facebook Ads depends on the individual's ad spend and the effectiveness of their ad campaigns. A person with a small budget and less effective ad campaigns is likely to earn less than someone with a higher budget and more effective ad campaigns.

To effectively use Facebook Ads to generate passive income, individuals should have a strong understanding of their target audience and be able to create engaging content that will attract and retain that audience. It's also important to keep up with changes and updates to Facebook's advertising policies and algorithms to ensure the best results.

Sponsored Tweets

Sponsored tweets are a way to generate passive income by leveraging your social media following. Essentially, companies will pay you to post tweets promoting their products or services to your followers. This is a popular method for businesses to increase their online presence and reach new customers.

To get started with sponsored tweets, you first need to build a following on Twitter. This means consistently posting engaging content and interacting with other users on the platform to grow your audience. Once you have a substantial following, you can begin to monetize your account through sponsored tweets.

Here are some tips for growing your Twitter following to increase opportunities for sponsored tweets:

1. *Optimize your profile*: Make sure your Twitter profile has a clear and professional photo, bio, and header image. This will help potential followers understand who you are and what you tweet about.
2. *Engage with others*: Respond to tweets, retweet content from others, and participate in Twitter chats and conversations related to your niche. This will help you get noticed by other Twitter users and potentially gain new followers.
3. *Share valuable content*: Tweet content that your followers will find interesting and valuable. This could be original content, curated content, or a mix of both. Sharing valuable content will help establish you as an authority in your niche and attract more followers.
4. *Use hashtags*: Hashtags help your tweets get discovered by people who are interested in the topics you're tweeting about. Use relevant hashtags in your tweets to increase visibility and attract new followers.
5. *Collaborate with other influencers*: Collaborating with other Twitter influencers in your niche can help you reach new

audiences and gain new followers. Consider hosting a Twitter chat or doing a guest tweet swap with another influencer.

6. ***Promote your Twitter account***: Promote your Twitter account on your website, blog, and other social media profiles. Make it easy for people to follow you on Twitter by including social media icons and links to your profile.

Here are some resources for finding sponsored tweet opportunities:

1. ***SponsoredTweets***: This is a platform that connects advertisers with Twitter users who are interested in making money by tweeting sponsored content.

2. ***PayPerPost***: This platform allows you to earn money by creating sponsored content on various social media platforms, including Twitter.

3. ***Revfluence***: This platform is designed for influencers who want to monetize their social media following. You can sign up for free and start browsing sponsored tweet opportunities.

4. ***IZEA:*** This platform connects influencers with brands looking for sponsored content across various social media channels, including Twitter.

5. ***Tomoson***: This platform connects influencers with brands and allows you to create sponsored content across various social media channels, including Twitter.

If you're considering using sponsored tweets for passive income, here are some things to be aware of:

1. ***Disclosure requirements***: If you're being paid to promote a product or service on Twitter, it's important to disclose that fact to your followers. The Federal Trade Commission (FTC) requires influencers to clearly disclose any sponsored content to avoid misleading their audience.

2. ***Target audience***: When considering sponsored tweets, it's important to think about your target audience and whether the sponsored content is relevant to them. If your followers are not interested in the product or service being promoted, the sponsored tweet may not be effective.

3. *Brand reputation*: Be selective about the products and services you promote on Twitter. Promoting a low-quality or controversial product could harm your reputation and credibility with your followers.
4. *Frequency*: Avoid bombarding your followers with too many sponsored tweets. Over-promotion could annoy your followers and cause them to unfollow you.
5. *Value proposition*: Consider whether the sponsored tweet provides value to your followers. If it's a product or service they may genuinely be interested in, they may appreciate your recommendation.
6. *Legal issues*: Be aware of legal issues such as copyright infringement and defamation when promoting products or services on Twitter. Make sure you have permission to use any images or content and avoid making false or misleading claims.
7. *Compensation*: It's important to negotiate fair compensation for your sponsored tweets. Consider the time and effort it takes to create the tweet and the value of your influence on Twitter.

The amount earned per month with sponsored tweets can vary greatly depending on several factors such as the individual's social media following, engagement rates, and the advertiser's budget. Generally, individuals with larger and engaged social media followings can command higher rates for sponsored tweets.

According to a survey by *IZEA*, the average rate for a sponsored tweet in 2020 was $0.10 to $0.30 per engagement (such as likes, comments, and retweets). Therefore, a tweet with 100 engagements could earn between $10 and $30. However, it's important to note that these are just estimates and many influencers negotiate their own rates with brands.

Additionally, the amount earned through sponsored tweets is dependent on the individual's ability to attract and engage with their followers, as well as their ability to promote products or services in an authentic way that resonates with their audience.

When crafting sponsored tweets, it's important to be transparent with your followers and clearly label the tweet as an advertisement. This helps to maintain trust with your audience and ensures compliance with advertising regulations. By participating in sponsored tweet campaigns, you can generate passive income while also promoting products and services that align with your personal brand and interests. It's a win-win situation for both you and the businesses you partner with.

Pinterest Affiliate Marketing

Pinterest affiliate marketing involves using Pinterest as a platform to promote products or services and earn commissions for any resulting sales. As a visual social media platform, Pinterest is ideal for promoting products, particularly those that can be showcased through images, such as fashion items, home decor, beauty products, and more.

To get started with Pinterest affiliate marketing, you'll need to create a Pinterest account and start building your following by creating and sharing high-quality content related to your niche. You can then join affiliate programs for products or services that align with your niche and share affiliate links to those products on your Pinterest boards.

When creating your boards, it's important to keep in mind the interests of your audience and curate boards that align with their interests. This will help attract more followers and increase the chances of them clicking on your affiliate links.

One of the most popular affiliate networks for Pinterest is the Amazon Associates program, which offers a wide range of products that can be promoted on Pinterest. Other popular affiliate networks include ShareASale, Commission Junction, and Rakuten Marketing.

To optimize your success with Pinterest affiliate marketing, it's important to keep up with current trends and use search engine optimization (SEO) techniques to ensure your pins are easily discoverable by users. You can also use tools such as Tailwind to schedule and automate your pinning activity.

If Pinterest affiliate marketing appeals to you as a source of passive income, here are some resources to help you:

1. *Pinterest's Affiliate Marketing Policy*: Before you start promoting affiliate products on Pinterest, be sure to read the platform's policy regarding affiliate marketing. This will ensure that you are following the rules and won't get your account suspended.

2. *Affiliate Networks*: Sign up with affiliate networks such as *ShareASale*, *Commission Junction*, and *Amazon Associates* to find products to promote on Pinterest. These networks allow you to earn a commission on sales that are made through your affiliate links.

3. *Pinterest Marketing Courses*: There are many courses available online that can help you learn how to use Pinterest for affiliate marketing. These courses cover everything from setting up your account to creating pins that convert to sales.

4. *Pinterest Marketing Tools*: Use tools like *Tailwind* and *BoardBooster* to schedule your pins and analyze your Pinterest performance. These tools can save you time and help you optimize your Pinterest strategy for maximum results.

5. *Affiliate Marketing Blogs*: Follow blogs such as *Smart Passive Income*, *Niche Pursuits*, and *Affilorama* to stay up to date on the latest affiliate marketing trends and strategies. These blogs offer valuable insights and tips for success in affiliate marketing.

If you're considering using Pinterest for affiliate marketing to earn passive income, here are some things to be aware of:

1. *FTC Disclosure Requirements*: As with any affiliate marketing program, it's important to disclose that you're using affiliate links on your Pinterest account to comply with the FTC's guidelines. This helps maintain transparency with your audience and avoid any legal issues.

2. *Pinterest's Acceptable Use Policy*: Pinterest has strict guidelines on what can and cannot be promoted on their platform, so it's important to review their Acceptable Use Policy to ensure that you're not promoting any prohibited content. Violating their policy can result in account suspension or even legal action.

3. *Quality Content*: To make your affiliate links more appealing to your followers, it's important to create quality content on your Pinterest account. This includes creating visually appealing pins, writing descriptive and engaging pin descriptions, and organizing your boards effectively.

4. *Affiliate Program Selection*: Choose affiliate programs that align with your niche or interests and ensure that the products or services you promote are high-quality and relevant to your audience. This will increase the likelihood of earning commissions from your links.

5. *Tracking and Analytics*: Use tools to track your clicks and conversions on your affiliate links to monitor their performance. This can help you identify which pins are generating the most traffic and commissions and adjust your strategies accordingly.

6. *Ethical Promotion*: Avoid over-promoting affiliate products or services to your followers, and only promote products or services that you genuinely believe in. Your followers will appreciate your authenticity and honesty, and it will build trust and credibility with your audience.

7. *Copyright Infringement*: Be aware of copyright infringement when creating and sharing content on Pinterest. Ensure that you have the rights to use any images or content and avoid using copyrighted material without permission.

The amount of money an average person can earn per month with Pinterest Affiliate Marketing depends on several factors, such as the niche, target audience, the number of followers, and the quality of the affiliate products being promoted. Generally, individuals with larger and engaged social media followings and who are in popular niches can command higher rates for affiliate marketing.

According to a survey by *Mediavine*, the average earnings per thousand impressions (EPM) for Pinterest in 2021 was $1.00 to $5.00. Therefore, if a person's pins receive 100,000 impressions per month, they could earn between $100 and $500 per month from affiliate marketing. However, these are just estimates and earnings can vary widely depending on the individual's niche, engagement rates, and the quality of the affiliate products being promoted.

Pinterest affiliate marketing can be a great way to generate passive income, particularly if you have a strong following and consistently share high-quality content that resonates with your audience.

Sponsored Blog Posts

Sponsored blog posts are one of the many ways bloggers can earn money through their websites. Essentially, a sponsored post is a blog post written by the blogger that is paid for by a company or advertiser. The blogger writes a post that promotes the company or its products, and in exchange, they are paid a fee.

To generate passive income through sponsored blog posts, bloggers need to build a large following and establish themselves as a reputable source of information in their niche. They can then attract advertisers who want to reach their audience and offer to write sponsored posts.

When writing sponsored blog posts, it's important for bloggers to disclose that the post is sponsored and to maintain their editorial integrity by only promoting products or services that they believe in and that are relevant to their audience.

Some resources for finding sponsored blog post opportunities include:

1. *Sponsored Content Marketplace*: This platform connects bloggers with brands looking for sponsored content opportunities.
2. *Blog Meets Brand*: This platform connects bloggers with brands looking to create sponsored content campaigns.
3. *IZEA*: This platform offers sponsored content opportunities, including sponsored blog posts, to influencers in a variety of niches.
4. *Linqia*: This platform offers sponsored content opportunities to bloggers with engaged audiences in specific niches.
5. *Social Fabric*: This platform offers sponsored content opportunities to bloggers in the food, parenting, and lifestyle niches.

There are several resources available online that can help bloggers create a media kit to showcase their blog's statistics and demographics to attract potential sponsors. Some of these resources include:

1. *Canva*: Canva is a popular graphic design tool that can be used to create professional-looking media kits. It offers a variety of customizable templates that can be easily edited to include blog statistics, demographics, and other relevant information.
2. *Google Analytics*: Google Analytics is a free web analytics service that provides detailed insights into website traffic and user behavior. Bloggers can use this tool to track their website's performance and include relevant statistics in their media kits.
3. *Social Blade*: Social Blade is a social media analytics platform that provides insights into a blogger's social media following and engagement. This information can be included in a media kit to showcase the blogger's reach and influence.
4. *Demographics Pro*: Demographics Pro is a social media analytics tool that provides detailed information about a blogger's audience demographics. This information can be used to create a targeted media kit that appeals to potential sponsors.
5. *Fohr*: Fohr is a platform that connects influencers with brands for sponsored content opportunities. It also provides a free media kit builder tool that bloggers can use to create professional-looking media kits.
6. *PitchKit*: PitchKit is a paid platform that offers customizable media kit templates and other tools to help bloggers pitch themselves to potential sponsors.
7. *Media Kit Smash*: Media Kit Smash is a free online tool that provides customizable media kit templates for bloggers. It also offers tips and resources to help bloggers create effective media kits.

The amount earned per month with sponsored blog posts can vary greatly depending on several factors such as the individual's blog niche, audience size, engagement rates, and the advertiser's budget. Generally, bloggers with larger and engaged audiences in popular niches can command higher rates for sponsored blog posts.

According to a survey by *Influence.co*, the average rate for a sponsored blog post in 2021 was $250 to $500 per post. However, rates can vary widely depending on the blogger's niche and the advertiser's budget.

Additionally, some bloggers negotiate their own rates with brands, so the rates can vary even further.

The amount earned through sponsored blog posts is also dependent on the blogger's ability to write high-quality content that resonates with their audience and effectively promotes the advertiser's products or services. Bloggers who can create high-quality sponsored content and promote it effectively to their audience are more likely to earn more from sponsored blog posts.

Sponsored blog posts can provide a steady stream of passive income through collaborations with brands and companies looking to promote their products or services to your audience. As always, the goal is to continue to grow your following and consistently share high-quality content that resonates with your audience.

Sponsored TikTok Posts

TikTok differs from other social media platforms in several ways. First, its primary focus is short-form video content, with a maximum length of 60 seconds. Second, its algorithm is designed to promote content based on user engagement, rather than just follower count, making it easier for users to gain visibility and followers. Third, TikTok's editing & effects tools make it easy for users to create engaging and visually appealing videos, even with limited experience in video editing. Finally, TikTok's user base tends to skew younger, with a large percentage of users under the age of 30, making it an attractive platform for brands targeting a younger demographic.

Sponsored TikTok posts can generate passive income by partnering with brands to create and promote content that aligns with their marketing goals. As a TikTok creator with a large following, you can use your platform to showcase products or services in a creative and engaging way.

By including a call-to-action and trackable link in your sponsored posts, you can earn commission on sales made through your content. TikTok's algorithm also promotes content that receives high engagement, so sponsored posts have the potential to reach a wider audience and generate more income.

Here are some resources for TikTok creators to generate passive income:

1. *TikTok Creator Fund*: TikTok offers a creator fund to its most popular creators. This program pays creators for their content based on the views and engagement they receive.
2. *Brand Deals*: Many brands are looking to collaborate with popular TikTok creators. Creators can approach brands or agencies to pitch their services, or they can sign up with influencer marketing platforms like *CreatorIQ*, *TRIBE*, and *HypeAuditor*.
3. *Merchandise Sales*: Creators can monetize their following by selling merchandise. TikTok recently launched a feature that allows creators to sell merchandise directly on the app.

4. *Live Streaming*: Creators can earn money through live streaming on TikTok. Viewers can buy virtual gifts and coins, which can be converted into real money.

5. *Affiliate Marketing*: Creators can earn commission by promoting products and services through affiliate marketing. They can sign up for affiliate programs with brands or use affiliate marketing platforms like *Amazon Associates* or *Skimlinks*.

6. *TikTok Creator Marketplace*: TikTok Creator Marketplace is a platform where creators can connect with brands and agencies looking for influencers. It offers creators opportunities to collaborate with brands and earn money for their content.

7. *Crowdfunding*: Creators can use crowdfunding platforms like *Patreon* to generate passive income. Fans can support their favorite creators by pledging a monthly amount in exchange for exclusive content and perks.

If you're considering using sponsored TikTok posts for passive income, here are some things to be aware of:

1. *Disclosure Requirements*: As with any sponsored content, it's important to disclose that you're being paid to promote a product or service on TikTok. This helps maintain transparency with your audience and avoid any legal issues.

2. *TikTok Guidelines*: TikTok has strict guidelines on what can and cannot be promoted on their platform, so it's important to review their guidelines to ensure that you're not promoting any prohibited content. Violating their guidelines can result in account suspension or even legal action.

3. *Target Audience*: It's important to ensure that the sponsored content is relevant to your target audience. If your followers are not interested in the product or service being promoted, the sponsored post may not be effective.

4. *Brand Reputation*: Be selective about the products and services you promote on TikTok. Promoting a low-quality or controversial product could harm your reputation and credibility with your followers.

5. *Frequency*: Avoid bombarding your followers with too many sponsored posts. Over-promotion could annoy your followers and cause them to unfollow you.
6. *Value Proposition*: Consider whether the sponsored post provides value to your followers. If it's a product or service they may genuinely be interested in, they may appreciate your recommendation.
7. *Legal Issues*: Be aware of legal issues such as copyright infringement and defamation when promoting products or services on TikTok. Make sure you have permission to use any images or content, and avoid making false or misleading claims.
8. *Compensation*: It's important to negotiate fair compensation for your sponsored TikTok posts. Consider the time and effort it takes to create the content and the value of your influence on TikTok.

The amount of money an average person can earn per month with sponsored TikTok posts depends on several factors such as the individual's TikTok following, engagement rates, and the advertiser's budget. Generally, individuals with larger and engaged TikTok followings can command higher rates for sponsored posts.

According to a survey by Influencer Marketing Hub, the average rate for a sponsored TikTok post in 2021 was $0.01 to $0.02 per view. Therefore, a sponsored TikTok post with 100,000 views could earn between $1,000 and $2,000. However, it's important to note that these are just estimates and many influencers negotiate their own rates with brands.

Additionally, the amount earned through sponsored TikTok posts is dependent on the individual's ability to attract and engage with their followers, as well as their ability to promote products or services in an authentic way that resonates with their audience.

Sponsored TikTok posts offer the potential for high engagement and viral reach, making it a lucrative platform for influencers and creators to generate passive income through brand partnerships.

Podcast Sponsorships

Podcast sponsorships are a great way to generate passive income if you have a popular podcast. Brands are always looking for ways to reach new audiences, and sponsoring a podcast is a great way to do that. Typically, podcast sponsorships involve the host promoting the brand's product or service in the middle of the episode. The host may read a pre-written ad or share their personal experience with the product. In exchange for the sponsorship, the brand pays the host a fee, which can range from a few hundred to several thousand dollars per episode.

To create a great podcast, you need a few essential pieces of equipment. Here's a list of what you'll need:

1. *Microphone*: A good-quality microphone is essential for recording clear and crisp audio. There are many microphones to choose from, ranging from USB microphones that plug directly into your computer to XLR microphones that require an audio interface.
2. *Headphones*: A good pair of headphones will help you hear yourself and your co-hosts more clearly, which is important for maintaining good audio quality.
3. *Audio interface*: If you're using an XLR microphone, you'll need an audio interface to connect your microphone to your computer.
4. *Recording software*: You'll need software to record and edit your podcast episodes. There are many options available, including *Audacity* (free), *GarageBand* (Mac only), *Adobe Audition*, and *Hindenburg Journalist*.
5. *Pop filter*: A pop filter helps to reduce popping sounds when you say words that start with "p" or "b."
6. *Mic stand or boom arm*: A mic stand or boom arm will help you position your microphone correctly and reduce unwanted noise caused by handling the microphone.
7. *Room treatment*: If you're recording in a room with hard surfaces, you may need to add some room treatment to reduce echo and other unwanted sounds.

To attract podcast sponsorships, it's important to have a significant and engaged audience. Brands are looking for podcasts that align with their values and target audience. It's also important to have a professional sounding podcast with good audio quality and consistent publishing schedule.

There are several podcast networks and agencies that connect podcasters with sponsors, as well as online marketplaces where you can list your podcast for potential sponsors to find. It's important to choose sponsorships that align with your brand and values to maintain authenticity and trust with your audience. Here are some resources for finding podcast sponsorships:

1. *Advertisecast*: This is a marketplace where podcasters can connect with potential sponsors.
2. *Midroll*: This is a podcast advertising network that connects advertisers with podcasters.
3. *Podcorn*: This platform allows podcasters to find sponsorships and collaborations with brands.
4. *Anchor*: This podcasting platform offers monetization opportunities, including sponsorships and listener support.
5. *Patreon*: This platform allows podcasters to receive monthly payments from their listeners, which can help support their podcast and generate passive income.
6. *Blueberry*: This is a podcast hosting platform that offers a monetization program for podcasters, including sponsorships.
7. *PodcastOne*: This is a podcast network that connects podcasters with advertisers.
8. *AdvertiseCast*: This is a platform that connects podcasters with advertisers, with options for dynamic ad insertion and targeted ad campaigns.
9. *Buzzsprout*: This podcast hosting platform offers a monetization program for podcasters, including sponsorships.
10. *Transistor*: This is a podcast hosting platform that offers a built-in sponsorship feature for podcasters to monetize their content.

The amount of money an average person can earn per month with podcast sponsorships depends on several factors such as the individual's podcast niche, audience size, engagement rates, and the advertiser's budget. Generally, podcasters with larger and engaged audiences in popular niches can command higher rates for sponsorships.

According to a survey by *Midroll*, the average rate for a 30-second ad on a podcast with 1,000 listeners is about $18. Therefore, a podcast with 10,000 listeners could earn about $180 per 30-second ad. However, rates can vary widely depending on the podcaster's niche and the advertiser's budget. Additionally, some podcasters negotiate their own rates with brands, so the rates can vary even further.

The amount earned through podcast sponsorships is also dependent on the podcaster's ability to create high-quality content that resonates with their audience and effectively promotes the advertiser's products or services. Podcasters who can create high-quality sponsored content and promote it effectively to their audience are more likely to earn more from sponsorships.

Podcast sponsorships provide a great opportunity for passive income through advertising revenue, while also building a loyal audience and establishing credibility in your niche. The objective remains the same: increase your followers and regularly post top-notch content that connects with your viewership.

Twitch Streaming

Twitch is a popular streaming platform where users can broadcast their live gameplay, creative content, and other activities to a global audience. Twitch streamers can earn passive income through various methods, including sponsorships, donations, and affiliate marketing.

Growing your viewership on Twitch takes time and effort, but here are some tips to get you started:

1. *Stream regularly*: Consistent streaming is key to building a loyal fanbase. Create a schedule and stick to it.
2. *Interact with your audience*: Engage with your viewers in the chat and make them feel valued. Respond to their comments and questions.
3. *Collaborate with other streamers*: Networking with other streamers can help you reach new audiences and build relationships in the community.
4. *Play games that are popular on Twitch*: Playing games that are popular on Twitch can help you get discovered by new viewers.
5. *Use social media*: Promote your stream on social media platforms like Twitter, Instagram, and Discord to reach new potential viewers.
6. *Offer giveaways and incentives*: Offering giveaways and other incentives can help you attract new viewers and keep your existing audience engaged.
7. *Invest in quality equipment*: A high-quality microphone, camera, and lighting setup can help make your stream look and sound more professional, which can help attract and retain viewers.
8. *Be yourself*: Authenticity is key on Twitch. Don't try to be someone you're not. Instead, be true to yourself and let your personality shine through.

One way to generate passive income on Twitch is through sponsorships. Brands can sponsor Twitch streamers by paying them to promote their products or services during their streams. This can include showing ads, using certain products during gameplay, or simply mentioning the brand.

Donations are another way for Twitch streamers to earn passive income. Viewers can donate money to their favorite streamers during their live streams, which can add up to a significant amount over time. Some Twitch streamers also use affiliate marketing to earn passive income by promoting products or services and earning a commission on any sales made through their unique affiliate links.

Here are some resources for Twitch streaming:

1. *Twitch Creator Camp*: This is an official Twitch resource that offers courses and tutorials on how to grow your channel, engage with your audience, and monetize your streams.
2. *Twitch Affiliate Program*: Once you meet the requirements, you can become a Twitch Affiliate and start earning revenue through subscriptions, ad revenue, and more.
3. *Streamlabs OBS*: This is a popular broadcasting software that can help you customize your stream and add overlays, alerts, and other features to enhance your audience's viewing experience.
4. *Discord*: This platform can be used to connect with your audience, build a community, and offer exclusive content and perks to your subscribers.
5. *Patreon*: This is a platform where fans can support their favorite creators by pledging a monthly subscription fee. As a Twitch streamer, you can offer exclusive content and perks to your Patreon supporters.
6. *YouTube*: You can use YouTube to create highlights and compilations of your Twitch streams, which can attract new viewers and help you build your following.
7. *Reddit*: There are many active communities on Reddit where you can share your streams, interact with other streamers, and engage with potential viewers.

If you're considering using Twitch streaming for passive income, here are some things to be aware of:

1. *Twitch Partner Program*: To earn passive income through Twitch, you need to be a Twitch Partner or Affiliate. The Twitch Partner Program has strict requirements for eligibility, including a certain

number of viewers, hours streamed, and consistency in your streaming schedule. It's important to meet these requirements to be considered for the program.

2. *Consistency*: To grow your audience and maintain a steady flow of passive income, it's important to stream regularly and consistently. This means sticking to a schedule and communicating any changes with your audience.

3. *Quality Content*: Creating high-quality and engaging content is key to growing your audience and earning passive income on Twitch. This includes having a clear brand and niche, using high-quality equipment, and being interactive with your audience.

4. *Fan Interaction*: Building a community and interacting with your fans is important for growing your audience and maintaining their loyalty. Responding to comments and engaging with your viewers can help build relationships and create a positive and supportive environment.

5. *Monetization*: There are various ways to monetize your Twitch stream, including ads, subscriptions, donations, sponsorships, and merchandise. It's important to consider which monetization strategies work best for your brand and audience, and to be transparent with your audience about any sponsored content.

6. *Legal Issues*: Be aware of legal issues when streaming on Twitch, such as copyright infringement, defamation, and privacy violations. Make sure you have permission to use any music or images, and avoid making false or misleading claims.

7. *Mental and Physical Health*: Streaming for long periods of time can have a negative impact on your mental and physical health. It's important to take breaks, prioritize self-care, and maintain a healthy work-life balance.

According to a 2021 survey by *Streamlabs* and *Stream Hatchet*, the average Twitch streamer earns approximately $2,400 per month. However, this figure varies widely, with some top Twitch streamers earning millions of dollars per year and many others earning very little or nothing at all.

Some of the factors that can influence the amount of money earned from Twitch streaming include:

1. ***Twitch following***: Twitch streamers with larger and engaged followings are more likely to earn more money, as they can attract more viewers, subscribers, and sponsors.

2. ***Average concurrent viewers***: The number of viewers watching a streamer's stream at any given time can affect their revenue. Streamers with more viewers are more likely to earn more money through ads, subscriptions, and donations.

3. ***Revenue streams***: The number and types of revenue streams utilized by a streamer can also impact their earnings. Streamers who use a variety of revenue streams, such as sponsorships and affiliate marketing, in addition to subscriptions and donations, are more likely to earn more money.

Twitch Streaming offers a unique opportunity for individuals with a passion for gaming and entertaining to generate passive income through sponsorships, donations, and affiliate marketing. By building a loyal following and consistently producing high-quality content, Twitch Streamers can turn their hobby into a lucrative source of passive income.

Chapter 7: Affiliate & Referral Marketing

Affiliate Marketing on LinkedIn

LinkedIn distinguishes itself from other social media platforms by being a professional networking site that focuses on connecting professionals. With a focus on building a professional brand, showcasing expertise, and networking, LinkedIn offers opportunities for affiliate marketing by promoting relevant products and services to a targeted audience. Affiliate marketing on LinkedIn involves promoting a product or service through your LinkedIn profile or company page and earning a commission for each sale made through your referral link.

To generate passive income through affiliate marketing on LinkedIn, you can build a following by consistently sharing valuable content related to your niche and industry, and then incorporate affiliate links within your posts or articles. For example, if you're a career coach, you can share articles about job searching or interview tips and include affiliate links for resume writing services or online courses.

Resources for Affiliate Marketing on LinkedIn include joining affiliate networks such *as CJ Affiliate*, *ShareASale*, or *Amazon Associates*, as well as researching companies in your niche that offer affiliate programs. You can also use *LinkedIn Analytics* to track your post engagement and refine your content strategy to attract more followers and potential customers. Additional resources include:

1. *LinkedIn Learning*: LinkedIn offers a range of courses on affiliate marketing, including *Affiliate Marketing Foundations* and *Advanced Affiliate Marketing*.
2. *Affiliate Marketing Groups*: LinkedIn has several groups dedicated to affiliate marketing, such as the Affiliate Marketing Network and Affiliate Marketers.
3. *Affiliate Marketing Platforms*: You can use affiliate marketing platforms like *ShareASale*, *CJ Affiliate*, and *Rakuten Marketing* to find affiliate programs that are relevant to your niche and promote them on LinkedIn.
4. *LinkedIn Ads*: You can also use LinkedIn Ads to promote affiliate products and services to your target audience on the platform.

5. ***LinkedIn Influencers***: Partnering with LinkedIn influencers in your niche can also help you promote affiliate products and increase your earnings.

According to some reports, the average earnings per click (EPC) for LinkedIn affiliate marketing can range from $0.50 to $5.00 or more per click, depending on the niche and products promoted. The commission rates can vary widely depending on the affiliate program, ranging from a few percent to over 50% of the sale value. However, these figures are just estimates, and the actual amount earned per month depends on various factors such as the individual's following, engagement rates, and the commission rates offered by the affiliate programs.

LinkedIn's professional network and focus on B2B interactions make it a prime platform for targeted affiliate marketing, offering a potentially lucrative source of passive income for those with relevant expertise.

Referral Marketing

Referral marketing is a type of marketing where you earn a commission or reward for promoting a product or service to others. As a passive income stream, referral marketing involves leveraging your existing network of contacts to promote products or services to them and receive a commission for any sales or conversions that result from your referrals.

To be successful in referral marketing, it is important to choose products or services that align with your values and interests, as this will make it easier for you to promote them to others. You should also focus on building relationships with your network and establishing trust, as people are more likely to take your recommendations seriously if they trust you and your opinions.

One popular way to get started with referral marketing is to join affiliate programs offered by companies that you use and love. These programs provide you with a unique referral link or code that you can share with your network. When someone clicks on your link or uses your code to make a purchase, you earn a commission on that sale.

Another option is to participate in referral programs offered by online platforms and apps, such as ride-sharing services, food delivery services, and peer-to-peer lending platforms. These programs often provide you with a referral code that you can share with friends and family, and you earn a commission when they sign up and use the service for the first time.

To maximize your earnings with referral marketing, it is important to be strategic in your approach. This includes targeting the right audience and promoting products and services that are relevant to them. It also involves being proactive in your outreach efforts, such as reaching out to people in your network who you think might be interested in the products or services you are promoting.

There are several resources you can use to find reputable referral marketing companies for passive income. Here are some options to consider:

1. ***ReferralExchange***: ReferralExchange is a real estate referral network that connects real estate agents and brokers across the US. You can sign up to become a member and receive referral commissions for any referrals you make.
2. ***Refersion***: Refersion is a referral marketing platform that helps businesses manage and track their referral programs. As a member, you can earn passive income by referring new customers to businesses that use Refersion.
3. ***ShareASale***: ShareASale is an affiliate marketing network that connects businesses with affiliate marketers. As a member, you can earn commissions by promoting products and services through your affiliate links.
4. ***Commission Junction***: Commission Junction is another affiliate marketing network that connects businesses with affiliate marketers. You can sign up to become an affiliate marketer and earn commissions by promoting products and services through your affiliate links.
5. ***Affiliate Window***: Affiliate Window is a global affiliate marketing network that connects businesses with affiliate marketers. You can sign up to become an affiliate marketer and earn commissions by promoting products and services through your affiliate links.
6. ***ClickBank***: ClickBank is a popular affiliate marketing network that specializes in digital products. As a member, you can promote digital products through your affiliate links and earn commissions on any sales made through those links.
7. ***Amazon Associates***: Amazon Associates is Amazon's affiliate marketing program. As a member, you can promote Amazon products through your affiliate links and earn commissions on any sales made through those links.

When selecting a referral marketing company to work with, it's important to do your research and choose a reputable company that has a track record of paying out commissions on time. Be sure to read reviews, check their Better Business Bureau rating, and verify their payment process before signing up.

To estimate how much you can earn with referral marketing, you can start by looking at the commission rates offered by the referral program you're interested in promoting. Some referral programs offer fixed rewards for each successful referral, while others offer a percentage commission on the sales generated through referrals.

Assuming you refer a product or service that offers a commission of 10% on sales and the product's average sale value is $100, if you refer 10 successful sales per month, you could earn $100 in commission per month. However, if you refer 100 successful sales per month, you could earn $1,000 in commission per month.

Referral marketing can be a great way to generate passive income by leveraging your existing network and promoting products and services that you believe in. With the right approach and strategy, you can earn a steady stream of income through referrals without having to actively sell or promote products daily.

Participate In Digital Goods Affiliate Marketing Programs

Participating in digital goods affiliate marketing programs can generate passive income by promoting and selling digital products, such as software, e-books, courses, and online memberships, to an online audience. As an affiliate marketer, you earn a commission for each sale made through your unique affiliate link, which tracks the referral source and credits you with the sale.

To participate in digital goods affiliate marketing programs, you need to find products and services that match your niche or audience and sign up for their affiliate program. Many digital goods providers have affiliate programs that are free to join and offer commissions ranging from 10% to 50% or more.

One of the most popular digital goods affiliate marketing programs is *Amazon Associates*, which allows you to earn commissions on any product sold on *Amazon.com* through your affiliate link. Another popular platform is *ClickBank*, which is a marketplace for digital products and offers a wide range of products in various niches.

To succeed in digital goods affiliate marketing, it is important to choose quality products that align with your audience's interests and needs and promote them in a way that provides value to your audience. This can be done through creating content such as blog posts, reviews, and tutorials that incorporate your affiliate links, or through social media and email marketing.

It is also important to stay up to date with the latest trends and best practices in digital goods affiliate marketing, and to continually analyze and optimize your marketing efforts for maximum results.

There are several resources to find digital goods affiliate marketing promotions, including:

1. *Affiliate Networks*: Affiliate networks are a great place to find digital goods affiliate programs. Some popular affiliate networks include *ShareASale*, *CJ Affiliate*, and *Rakuten Marketing*.

2. *Digital Product Marketplaces*: Digital product marketplaces like *ClickBank*, *JVZoo*, and *WarriorPlus* offer affiliate programs for digital products such as software, courses, ebooks, and more.

3. *Online Marketplaces*: Online marketplaces like *Amazon*, *eBay*, and *Etsy* offer affiliate programs for digital goods like e-books, music, and videos.

4. *Social Media*: Social media platforms like *Twitter*, *Facebook*, and *Instagram* are great places to find affiliate marketing promotions for digital goods. Many digital product creators and marketers promote their affiliate programs on social media.

5. *Niche Websites*: Niche websites focused on a specific topic or industry often have affiliate marketing programs for relevant digital goods. For example, a technology website may have affiliate programs for software products, or a fitness website may have affiliate programs for online workout programs.

6. *Affiliate Marketing Directories*: Affiliate marketing directories like *Affilorama* and *AffiliatePrograms.com* offer directories of various affiliate programs, including those for digital goods.

If you're considering using digital goods affiliate marketing programs for passive income, here are some things to be aware of:

1. *Product Quality*: The success of your affiliate marketing efforts will depend on the quality of the digital goods you promote. It's important to research and evaluate the products you promote to ensure that they are of high quality and offer value to your audience.

2. *Audience Relevance*: Promoting digital goods that are relevant to your audience is key to earning passive income through affiliate marketing. Make sure the products you promote align with the interests and needs of your audience.

3. *Affiliate Program Requirements*: Different affiliate programs have different requirements for eligibility and compensation. It's important to review the requirements and terms of each program

before signing up to ensure that they align with your goals and expectations.

4. ***Promotion Methods***: There are various ways to promote digital goods as an affiliate, including through blog posts, social media, email marketing, and paid advertising. It's important to choose promotion methods that align with your brand and audience, and to avoid spamming or over-promoting.

5. ***Commission Rates***: Commission rates for digital goods affiliate programs vary, and it's important to evaluate the commission rates and compensation structure of each program to ensure that it aligns with your goals and expectations.

6. ***Disclosure Requirements***: It's important to disclose your affiliate relationship when promoting digital goods to maintain transparency with your audience and avoid legal issues.

7. ***Brand Reputation***: The digital goods you promote as an affiliate can impact your brand reputation and credibility. It's important to be selective about the products you promote and to avoid promoting low-quality or controversial products.

8. ***Payment Processing***: Different affiliate programs have different payment processing procedures, and it's important to review the payment terms and methods of each program before signing up.

The commission rates for digital goods affiliate marketing programs can vary widely, ranging from a few percent to over 50% of the sale value. Assuming a commission rate of 30% and a product's sale value of $100, if you refer 10 successful sales per month, you could earn $300 in commission per month. However, if you refer 100 successful sales per month, you could earn $3,000 in commission per month.

The actual amount earned per month with digital goods affiliate marketing programs varies widely and depends on various factors such as the individual's network size, engagement rates, and the commission rates offered by the affiliate programs.

Research and evaluate each affiliate program before joining to ensure it aligns with your interests and goals and offers a fair commission structure and reliable payment system.

Participate In Network Marketing Programs

Network marketing, also known as multi-level marketing (MLM), is a business model that allows individuals to earn money by promoting and selling products to others. In a network marketing program, you are not only selling products, but also recruiting other individuals to join the program and become part of your network or downline.

To participate in a network marketing program, you typically need to purchase a starter kit or an initial set of products to sell. You then earn a commission on the products you sell, as well as on the sales made by those you recruit into the program.

One of the key benefits of participating in a network marketing program is the potential for passive income. As you build your downline and your team of sales representatives grows, you can earn a percentage of the sales they make as well. This allows you to earn money even when you're not actively selling products or recruiting new members.

Another benefit of network marketing is the support and training provided by the company and your upline. Most network marketing companies offer resources and training to help you succeed in the business, including product information, marketing materials, and sales strategies. Additionally, your upline or sponsor can provide guidance and support as you navigate the business.

When selecting a network marketing company to participate in, there are a few things to be wary of to ensure that you don't fall prey to a scam or pyramid scheme. Here are some red flags to watch out for:

1. High-pressure sales tactics: If a company is pushing you to make a quick decision or invest a large sum of money upfront, this could be a sign that they are more interested in taking your money than in helping you succeed.
2. Focus on recruitment over product sales: If the main focus of the company seems to be on recruiting new members rather than

selling their products or services, this is a red flag. Legitimate network marketing companies should be primarily concerned with product sales, not just signing up new members.

3. Lack of transparency: If a company is not upfront about their compensation plan or other important details, this is cause for concern. You should have a clear understanding of how you will be compensated and what is expected of you as a member.

4. Unrealistic promises: If a company is making promises of quick and easy riches, this is likely too good to be true. Success in network marketing requires hard work, dedication, and a willingness to learn and grow.

5. Negative reviews or press: Before joining a network marketing company, do your research. Look for reviews from other members and news articles that discuss the company's practices. If there are many negative reviews or articles, this could be a warning sign.

Here are some things to be aware of when considering network marketing for passive income:

1. *Legitimacy*: There are many legitimate network marketing programs, but unfortunately, there are also many scams out there. It's essential to research and thoroughly vet any MLM opportunity before investing your time and money.

2. *Recruitment*: MLMs often focus heavily on recruitment, which can lead to pressure to bring in more people to the business. Make sure you are comfortable with the amount of recruitment required and that you're not being pressured to recruit beyond your comfort level.

3. *Costs*: MLMs often require an initial investment to join, as well as ongoing fees for training and materials. Be aware of all costs associated with the MLM and whether they align with your financial goals.

4. *Selling*: MLMs require members to sell products or services to earn commissions. Make sure you're comfortable with the product or service you're selling and that you believe in it. Also, consider if the product or service is unique and not readily available elsewhere.

5. *Time investment*: MLMs require a significant time investment to be successful, and the income earned is often directly related to the amount of time put in. Consider if you have the time and dedication required to make a meaningful income from the MLM.

The income potential in network marketing programs is often marketed as unlimited, but the reality is that most participants earn a modest income, and only a small percentage earn a significant income. The amount earned per month in network marketing depends largely on the size and activity of your network, as well as your own sales and recruiting efforts.

According to a survey by the *Direct Selling Association*, the median annual income for network marketing participants in the United States was $2,400, with the majority earning less than $1,000 per year. However, some successful network marketers earn six-figure incomes or more.

It's important to approach network marketing opportunities with caution and do your due diligence before investing your time and money. However, there are many legitimate network marketing companies out there that can provide a lucrative source of passive income for those who are willing to put in the effort.

Chapter 8:
Miscellaneous Passive
Income Ideas

Writing Reviews

Reviews are evaluations of products, services, or experiences, typically shared publicly on websites, social media platforms, or other media. Reviews can range from short comments to in-depth analysis and can be written in various formats, such as text, video, or audio.

Reviews can influence consumer behavior, as they provide valuable insights into the quality, features, and benefits of a product or service. Positive reviews can increase sales and brand loyalty, while negative reviews can hurt a company's reputation and sales.

Writing reviews can be a lucrative source of passive income for those with a flair for writing and a willingness to share their opinions. To write reviews that generate passive income, consider the following tips:

1. *Be honest and authentic*: Readers value authenticity and honesty, so be sure to share your true opinions and experiences. Don't be afraid to point out both the positive and negative aspects of a product or service.

2. *Provide detailed and helpful information*: Readers want to know the details of a product or service, such as its features, benefits, and drawbacks. Provide as much information as possible to help readers make informed decisions.

3. *Write in a clear and engaging style*: Reviews should be easy to read and engaging. Use clear and concise language and consider adding visuals, such as images or videos, to enhance your review.

4. *Build a following*: To increase your passive income potential, build a following of readers who trust your opinions and value your reviews. Share your reviews on social media and other platforms to reach a wider audience.

5. *Ethics and Transparency*: It's important to maintain ethics and transparency when writing reviews. This includes disclosing any sponsored content, avoiding false or misleading claims, and being honest about your opinions and experiences with the products you review.

6. *Legal Issues*: Be aware of legal issues when writing reviews, such as copyright infringement, defamation, and privacy violations. Make sure you have permission to use any images or media, and avoid making false or misleading claims.

7. *Reputation Management*: The reviews you write can impact your brand reputation and credibility. It's important to be selective about the products you review and to avoid promoting low-quality or controversial products.

Here are some resources for writing reviews to help generate passive income:

1. *Amazon Affiliate Program* - Amazon offers an affiliate program where you can earn a commission by writing reviews of products sold on their site. You can sign up for the program and create affiliate links to products, which you can then include in your reviews.

2. *Yelp Elite* - Yelp is a popular platform for reviews of local businesses. Yelp offers an Elite program for its most active and influential reviewers. As a Yelp Elite member, you can get exclusive invitations to events and free products, which can help you generate passive income.

3. *Google Local Guides* - Google Local Guides is a program where you can write reviews of local businesses and earn points for your contributions. These points can be redeemed for rewards, such as free Google Drive storage or Google Play credits.

4. *Software and App Review Sites* - There are many software and app review sites that pay you to write reviews of new apps and software products. Some examples include *SoftwareJudge.com*, *UserTesting.com*, and *ReviewStream.com*.

5. *Freelance Writing* - Freelance writing is a great way to earn passive income by writing reviews for various publications. You can write reviews for blogs, magazines, and other websites. You can also find freelance writing opportunities on job boards like *Upwork* or *Freelancer*.

6. *Sponsored Reviews* - Sponsored reviews are reviews that you are paid to write by a company or brand. You can find opportunities

for sponsored reviews by reaching out to companies directly or by signing up for sponsored review platforms like *PayPerPost* or *SponsoredReviews.com*.

7. ***Book Reviews*** - You can also earn passive income by writing book reviews for websites like ***Goodreads*** or ***Amazon***. You can also reach out to publishers directly to see if they are looking for book reviewers.

The pay rate for writing reviews can vary widely between platforms and products, with some platforms paying just a few cents per review and others paying several dollars or more. Assuming a pay rate of $1 per review and the ability to write 10 reviews per hour, you could potentially earn $100 per month writing reviews for an hour a day.

However, it's important to note that the actual amount earned per month writing reviews can vary widely and depends on various factors such as the quality of your reviews, the frequency of available review opportunities, and the demand for reviews on the platform.

Writing reviews can be an excellent source of passive income for those with a talent for writing and a willingness to share their opinions. By following the tips above and exploring the various ways to monetize your reviews, you can turn your passion for writing into a profitable venture.

Pet Sitting

Pet sitting is a type of business that involves taking care of pets in the absence of their owners. It is a great way to generate passive income because it is a service that people need on a regular basis, and pet owners are often willing to pay a premium for a reliable and trustworthy pet sitter.

There are several ways to get started with pet sitting as a source of passive income. One of the easiest ways is to advertise your services locally, either through flyers, word-of-mouth, or online platforms such as *Craigslist* or *Facebook Marketplace*. You can also consider registering with a pet sitting service or app, such as *Rover* or *Wag*, which can help you connect with pet owners in your area. Additional resources include:

1. *Care.com* - Care.com is a platform that connects families with caregivers, including pet sitters. You can sign up as a pet sitter and set your own rates. Care.com also handles the payment and insurance for you.
2. *PetSitter.com* - PetSitter.com is a platform that connects pet owners with pet sitters. You can sign up to become a pet sitter and set your own rates. PetSitter.com also provides resources and tools to help you manage your pet sitting business.
3. *PetBacker* - PetBacker is a global platform that connects pet owners with pet sitters, dog walkers, and other pet-related services. You can sign up to become a pet sitter and set your own rates. PetBacker handles the payment and insurance for you.
4. *Professional Associations* - Consider joining a professional pet-sitting association, such as the National Association of Professional Pet Sitters (NAPPS) or *Pet Sitters International* (PSI). These organizations provide resources and support for pet sitters, including training, certification, and networking opportunities.

Once you have established your pet sitting business, there are several ways to make it more passive. One way is to offer overnight pet sitting services, which can allow you to earn income while you sleep. You can also consider hiring additional pet sitters to work for you, which can help you scale your business and earn more income without having to take on more work yourself. Another way to make pet sitting more passive is to offer additional services such as dog walking, pet grooming, or even house sitting. These services can help you earn additional income from your existing client base and can also help you attract new clients who are looking for a full-service pet care provider.

The amount of money you can make pet sitting varies depending on various factors such as your location, the number and type of pets you care for, and the duration of each pet sitting job. According to data from *Care.com*, the average pay rate for a pet sitter in the United States is around $12.50 to $17.50 per hour. Assuming you work for an average of 20 hours per week, you could potentially earn around $1,000 to $1,400 per month pet sitting. The actual amount earned per month pet sitting, however, can vary widely and depends on various factors such as your experience, availability, and the demand for pet sitters in your area. Some pet sitters may also charge more for specialized services such as caring for exotic pets or providing overnight care.

Carefully screen and evaluate clients before accepting pet sitting jobs, as some clients may have difficult pets or unrealistic expectations. You should also have the appropriate insurance and licensing to protect yourself and the pets in your care.

Pet sitting does require some initial investment, including the cost of advertising, pet supplies, and any necessary training or certifications. However, once you have established your business and built up a client base, pet sitting can be a great source of passive income that requires minimal effort on your part.

House Sitting

House sitting can be a great way to earn passive income by providing a valuable service to homeowners who need someone to look after their homes while they are away. House sitters are responsible for taking care of the home, ensuring its safety, and performing various tasks such as feeding pets, watering plants, and keeping the house clean and tidy.

House sitting opportunities can come in different forms, such as short-term or long-term assignments, local or international house sitting, and paid or unpaid positions. Some homeowners may offer compensation for the house-sitting service, while others may provide free accommodation in exchange for the service.

To get started with house sitting as a passive income source, one can join online platforms that connect house sitters with homeowners seeking their services. Some popular platforms for house sitters allow house sitters to create a profile and list their availability, skills, and experience, while homeowners can search for suitable candidates based on their criteria. Here are some of the more popular options:

1. *TrustedHousesitters.com*: This is a platform that connects house sitters with homeowners who need someone to look after their property and pets while they are away.
2. *MindMyHouse.com*: This is another house-sitting platform that allows homeowners to find reliable and trustworthy house sitters to take care of their homes and pets.
3. *HouseSitter.com*: This platform connects homeowners with house sitters across the globe, offering a range of house-sitting opportunities that can help generate passive income.
4. *Nomador.com*: This website offers house sitting opportunities worldwide, including caring for pets and maintaining homes while homeowners are away.
5. *HouseCarers.com*: This is a platform where homeowners can find house sitters to take care of their homes and pets while they are away, and house sitters can find house sitting opportunities to generate passive income.

6. *Care.com*: While not specifically for house sitting, Care.com offers a range of pet care and housekeeping services, which could include house sitting as part of the services provided.
7. *Rover.com*: This platform offers a range of pet care services, including dog walking, pet sitting, and house sitting, which can help generate passive income for those interested in providing these services.
8. *Craigslist*: Local classifieds websites like Craigslist can be a useful resource for finding house sitting opportunities in your area.

If you're considering house sitting for passive income, here are some things to be aware of:

1. *Responsibility*: House sitting involves taking care of someone's home and pets, so it's important to take the responsibility seriously. Make sure you understand the homeowner's expectations and are comfortable with the tasks involved.
2. *Experience and References:* Many homeowners prefer house sitters who have experience and references. If you're new to house sitting, it may be helpful to start with friends or family members to gain experience and build your references.
3. *Communication*: Communication is key when house sitting. Make sure you establish clear communication with the homeowner before and during the house-sitting period and keep them updated on any issues or concerns.
4. *Insurance*: It's important to make sure you have the appropriate insurance coverage when house sitting. Some homeowners may require proof of insurance, so be prepared to provide this information if necessary.
5. *Legal Issues*: Be aware of legal issues when house sitting, such as liability and property damage. Make sure you have a clear agreement with the homeowner about any responsibilities and liabilities and consider consulting a lawyer if necessary.
6. *Availability*: House sitting may not always be available, as it depends on the homeowner's schedule and travel plans. Make sure you have alternative sources of income and a flexible schedule if you plan to rely on house sitting for passive income.

7. ***Background Checks***: Some homeowners may require background checks or other screening processes before hiring a house sitter. Be prepared to provide this information if necessary.

8. ***Reputation Management***: The house-sitting community is relatively small, so it's important to maintain a positive reputation and build relationships with homeowners. Be reliable, communicative, and respectful of the homeowner's property and privacy.

The amount of money you can make house sitting varies depending on various factors such as your location, the duration of each house-sitting job, and the responsibilities involved.

According to data from Care.com, the average pay rate for a house sitter in the United States is around $25 to $30 per day. Assuming you work for an average of 10 days per month, you could potentially earn around $250 to $300 per month house sitting.

However, it's important to note that the actual amount earned per month house sitting can vary widely and depends on various factors such as your experience, availability, and the demand for house sitters in your area. Some house sitters may also charge more for specialized services such as caring for pets or performing additional tasks such as cleaning or gardening.

Additionally, it's important to carefully screen and evaluate clients before accepting house sitting jobs, as some clients may have specific requirements or expectations. It's also important to have appropriate insurance and licensing to protect yourself and the property in your care.

House sitting can be a rewarding and flexible way to earn passive income while providing a valuable service to homeowners in need of a trustworthy and reliable house sitter. With the availability of online platforms and resources, it has never been easier to start earning passive income through house sitting. Remember to do your research and carefully vet any house-sitting opportunities or platforms before committing to them.

Dog Walking

Dog walking is a great way to earn passive income while enjoying the company of furry friends. As a dog walker, you'll typically be responsible for picking up dogs from their owners' homes and taking them for a walk or a run around the neighborhood. Depending on the length and frequency of walks, dog walkers can make a significant amount of money each month.

One of the advantages of dog walking as a passive income stream is that you don't need to invest a lot of money to get started. All you need is some experience with dogs, a love for animals, and the ability to walk or run for an extended period of time. It's also a very flexible job that you can easily fit around other commitments.

To get started with dog walking, you can create profiles on popular websites and apps like **PetBacker**. These platforms connect dog owners with local dog walkers and sitters, and you can earn money for each walk you complete. You can set your own rates and availability, and some platforms even offer additional services like overnight dog sitting and dog grooming. Here are some additional resources for dog walking as a passive income:

1. **Rover**: Rover is a website that connects dog owners with local dog sitters and walkers. You can create a profile as a dog walker and set your own rates. Rover also provides insurance and 24/7 support for its walkers.
2. **Wag!**: Wag! is a mobile app that connects dog owners with local dog walkers. As a walker, you can set your own schedule and rates, and Wag! provides liability insurance and support.
3. **PetSitter.com**: PetSitter.com is a website that connects pet owners with local pet sitters, including dog walkers. You can create a profile and list your services, rates, and availability.
4. **Care.com**: Care.com is a website that connects families with caregivers, including pet sitters and dog walkers. You can create a profile and apply to dog walking jobs in your area.

5. *Local advertising*: Consider advertising your dog walking services in local newspapers, on community bulletin boards, or by distributing flyers in your neighborhood.
6. *Referrals*: Ask your current clients to refer their friends and family to your dog walking services. Word of mouth is a powerful tool for growing your client base.
7. *Professional development*: Consider taking courses or workshops to improve your dog walking skills and knowledge. This can help you attract more clients and charge higher rates.

Networking in your local community is also a great way to find dog walking clients. You can advertise your services on social media platforms like Facebook and Instagram, as well as through word-of-mouth referrals from friends and family.

If you're considering dog walking for passive income, here are some things to be aware of:

1. *Dog Handling Skills*: Dog walking requires basic dog handling skills, such as understanding dog behavior, leash handling, and basic commands. Make sure you're comfortable working with dogs before offering dog walking services.
2. *Physical Demands*: Dog walking can be physically demanding, as it involves walking and potentially running with dogs. Make sure you're physically capable of handling the demands of the job.
3. *Safety*: Safety is a top priority when working with dogs. Make sure you have a plan in place for emergencies, such as a lost dog or injury, and make sure you're familiar with the area where you'll be walking dogs.
4. *Liability Insurance*: It's important to have liability insurance when offering dog walking services. This can protect you in case of any accidents or incidents that may occur while walking dogs.
5. *Licensing and Permitting*: Some cities or states may require licensing or permitting for dog walkers. Be aware of any local regulations and make sure you're in compliance.
6. *Availability*: Dog walking may not always be available, as it depends on the dog owner's schedule and needs. Make sure you

have alternative sources of income and a flexible schedule if you plan to rely on dog walking for passive income.

7. *Background Checks*: Some dog owners may require background checks or other screening processes before hiring a dog walker. Be prepared to provide this information if necessary.

8. *Reputation Management*: Building a positive reputation and relationships with dog owners is important for earning repeat business and referrals. Be reliable, communicative, and respectful of the dog and owner's needs.

The amount of money you can make dog walking varies depending on various factors such as your location, the number of dogs you walk, and the duration of each dog walking session. According to data from *Care.com*, the average pay rate for a dog walker in the United States is around $15 to $20 per hour. Assuming you work for an average of 20 hours per week, you could potentially earn around $1,200 to $1,600 per month dog walking.

However, it's important to note that the actual amount earned per month dog walking can vary widely and depends on various factors such as your experience, availability, and the demand for dog walkers in your area. Some dog walkers may also charge more for specialized services such as walking multiple dogs or providing additional services such as feeding or administering medication.

Additionally, it's important to carefully screen and evaluate clients before accepting dog walking jobs, as some dogs may have specific requirements or behavioral issues. It's also important to have appropriate insurance and licensing to protect yourself and the dogs in your care.

Dog walking can be a profitable and flexible way to earn passive income while also providing a valuable service to pet owners. With a low start-up cost, it can be a great option for those looking to supplement their income without committing to a full-time job.

Babysitting

Babysitting can be a lucrative source of passive income for individuals who enjoy working with children. Parents are always in need of reliable and trustworthy babysitters, which means that there is a consistent demand for this service. Babysitters can work part-time or full-time, and they can set their own rates based on their experience and location.

One way to generate passive income as a babysitter is to establish a network of clients who will regularly use your services. This can be done by advertising your services through social media, community boards, and word-of-mouth. As you build your reputation and gain more clients, you can increase your rates and potentially even hire additional babysitters to work under you.

Another option is to offer overnight babysitting services. Many parents need overnight care for their children, either for work-related reasons or for personal events such as weddings or vacations. By offering overnight babysitting services, you can charge higher rates and potentially earn more passive income.

It's important to note that babysitting requires a high level of responsibility and trustworthiness, as you are responsible for the safety and well-being of someone else's child. It's important to have a thorough understanding of first aid and emergency procedures, as well as good communication skills with both children and parents.

If babysitting interests you, here are several resources to find work and promote your services:

1. *Care.com*: This is a popular platform for babysitters to create a profile, advertise their services, and connect with potential clients.
2. *Sittercity*: This is another platform where babysitters can create a profile and apply to job listings. It also offers features such as background checks and scheduling tools.
3. *UrbanSitter*: This platform connects babysitters with families in their local area and offers features such as online booking and in-app payments.

4. **Word-of-mouth referrals**: Babysitters can also promote their services through word-of-mouth referrals from satisfied clients. This can be especially effective in local communities and neighborhoods.
5. **Social media**: Babysitters can use social media platforms such as Facebook and Instagram to promote their services and share their availability with their network.
6. **Local classifieds**: Babysitters can also advertise their services through local classifieds, such as community bulletin boards or classified ads in local newspapers.

If you're considering babysitting for passive income, here are some things to be aware of:

1. **Responsibility**: Babysitting involves caring for someone's children, so it's important to take the responsibility seriously. Make sure you understand the parents' expectations and are comfortable with the tasks involved.
2. **Experience and References**: Many parents prefer babysitters who have experience and references. If you're new to babysitting, it may be helpful to start with friends or family members to gain experience and build your references.
3. **Safety**: Safety is a top priority when caring for children. Make sure you're familiar with basic safety procedures, such as first aid and CPR, and make sure you have a plan in place for emergencies.
4. **Liability Insurance**: It's important to have liability insurance when offering babysitting services. This can protect you in case of any accidents or incidents that may occur while caring for children.
5. **Licensing and Permitting**: Some cities or states may require licensing or permitting for babysitters. Be aware of any local regulations and make sure you're in compliance.
6. **Availability**: Babysitting may not always be available, as it depends on the parents' schedule and needs. Make sure you have alternative sources of income and a flexible schedule if you plan to rely on babysitting for passive income.

7. ***Background Checks***: Some parents may require background checks or other screening processes before hiring a babysitter. Be prepared to provide this information if necessary.

8. ***Reputation Management***: Building a positive reputation and relationships with parents is important for earning repeat business and referrals. Be reliable, communicative, and respectful of the children and parents' needs.

The amount of money you can make babysitting varies depending on various factors such as your location, the number of children you're caring for, and the duration of each babysitting session.

According to data from ***Care.com***, the average pay rate for a babysitter in the United States is around $15 to $18 per hour for one child, and around $20 to $25 per hour for two or more children. Assuming you work for an average of 20 hours per week, you could potentially earn around $1,200 to $1,800 per month babysitting one child, or around $1,600 to $2,500 per month babysitting multiple children.

However, it's important to note that the actual amount earned per month babysitting can vary widely and depends on various factors such as your experience, availability, and the demand for babysitters in your area. Some babysitters may also charge more for specialized services such as caring for infants or children with special needs.

Additionally, it's important to carefully screen and evaluate clients before accepting babysitting jobs, as some children may have specific requirements or behavioral issues. It's also important to have appropriate insurance and licensing to protect yourself and the children in your care.

Babysitting can be a rewarding way to earn passive income, as there is a constant demand for reliable and trustworthy caregivers. With the right experience, training, and references, babysitters can build a reputation and earn a steady stream of income from families in need of their services. Additionally, babysitting allows for a flexible schedule and the opportunity to work with children, making it a fulfilling choice for those looking to generate passive income.

Personal Shopping

Personal shopping is a lucrative way to make passive income. It is a service that entails helping clients purchase clothes, accessories, or other personal items that meet their needs and preferences. Personal shoppers often work with clients who have a busy schedule or limited time to shop for themselves.

To generate passive income from personal shopping, you can offer your services online through a website, social media platforms, or by advertising in local publications. You can also leverage e-commerce platforms to build a personal shopping business. For instance, Amazon provides an affiliate program that enables you to earn commissions on every sale made through your referral link.

To get started with personal shopping, you will need to have good communication skills, an eye for fashion, and an understanding of your client's needs. You should be able to provide recommendations on clothing styles, colors, and accessories that complement your client's personality and body shape.

Additionally, it is important to build relationships with your clients by offering excellent customer service. This can include providing personalized recommendations, following up on previous purchases, and keeping in touch with them to offer new products or services.

To maximize your passive income from personal shopping, you can consider partnering with other businesses or influencers in the fashion industry. For example, you can collaborate with clothing stores, fashion bloggers, or social media influencers to promote your services to their followers. This can help you reach a larger audience and increase your chances of generating more sales.

If you're interested in personal shopping as a means of generating passive income, here are some additional resources for you to explore:

1. *Stylist School Online*: This website offers a comprehensive course on personal styling and shopping, covering everything from fashion trends to business skills.
2. *National Association of Personal Stylists*: This organization provides training, certification, and networking opportunities for personal stylists and shoppers.
3. *Stitch Fix*: This online styling service hires personal stylists to curate clothing and accessory options for their clients.
4. *Trunk Club*: This Nordstrom-owned service employs personal stylists to create custom clothing boxes for clients based on their preferences and needs.
5. *Online marketplaces*: Platforms like *Etsy*, *eBay*, and *Amazon* allow individuals to sell their personal shopping services to a global audience.
6. *Social media*: Personal shoppers can use social media platforms like Instagram to showcase their styling skills and attract clients.
7. *Personal website*: A personal website or blog can be used to showcase one's personal shopping services, share styling tips, and attract clients.
8. *Referral networks*: Personal shoppers can join referral networks or affiliate programs to earn commissions on purchases made by their clients.

The amount of money you can make as a personal shopper can vary widely depending on various factors such as your location, level of experience, and the type of clients you work with.

According to data from *Payscale*, the average hourly rate for a personal shopper in the United States is around $14 to $27 per hour, with the average annual salary ranging from around $23,000 to $88,000 per year.

Assuming you work for an average of 20 hours per week, you could potentially earn around $1,120 to $2,160 per month as a personal shopper, depending on your hourly rate and the number of clients you work with.

However, it's important to note that the actual amount earned per month as a personal shopper can vary widely and depends on various factors such as your level of experience, reputation, and the demand for personal shopping services in your area. Some personal shoppers may also charge more for specialized services such as wardrobe consulting or personal styling.

Additionally, it's important to carefully evaluate clients and establish clear boundaries and expectations before accepting personal shopping jobs, as some clients may have specific requirements or high demands. It's also important to have appropriate liability insurance and licensing to protect yourself and your clients.

Personal shopping is a great way to make passive income by offering a service that people need. With the right skills, communication, and marketing strategies, you can create a successful personal shopping business that generates consistent passive income.

Mystery Shopping

If you enjoy shopping and have an eye for detail, mystery shopping can be a great way to earn passive income. Mystery shopping involves visiting a store, restaurant, or other business anonymously to evaluate customer service, cleanliness, and other aspects of the customer experience. Here's how mystery shopping can generate passive income:

To get started with mystery shopping, you can sign up with a mystery shopping company. There are many companies that hire mystery shoppers, and you can find them by searching online or through referral from friends or acquaintances. Once you sign up with a company, you can browse available opportunities in your area.

Once you accept a mystery shopping assignment, you'll need to complete it within the designated timeframe. This may involve making a purchase, asking questions, or completing a survey. After the assignment, you'll need to submit a detailed report that includes your observations and feedback.

As a mystery shopper, you'll typically receive payment for your time and any purchases you make during the assignment. Payment can vary based on the company and the assignment, but typically ranges from $5 to $50 per assignment.

As you gain experience as a mystery shopper, you can build relationships with clients who may offer you additional assignments in the future. This can lead to a steady stream of passive income as you continue to complete mystery shopping assignments on a regular basis.

Some reputable mystery shopping organizations include:

1. *Mystery Shopping Providers Association* (MSPA): The MSPA is a trade organization for the mystery shopping industry. They provide resources and information for both mystery shopping companies and shoppers.

2. *Market Force*: Market Force is a leading mystery shopping company that offers a variety of assignments in different industries.

3. *BestMark*: BestMark is another reputable mystery shopping company that offers a range of assignments across the United States and Canada.

4. *Secret Shopper*: Secret Shopper is a mystery shopping company that offers opportunities in the retail, restaurant, and service industries.

If you're considering mystery shopping for passive income, here are some things to be aware of:

1. *Legitimacy*: Be aware of scams and only work with legitimate mystery shopping companies. Do your research and make sure the company is reputable before signing up.

2. *Time and Effort*: Mystery shopping requires time and effort, as you'll need to complete assignments and write reports. Make sure you're able to commit the time and effort required for the job.

3. *Expenses*: Some mystery shopping assignments may require you to purchase items or services, such as a meal at a restaurant or a haircut at a salon. Make sure you're aware of any expenses involved and factor them into your earnings.

4. *Payment*: Some mystery shopping companies may pay in cash, while others may offer reimbursements or gift cards. Make sure you're comfortable with the payment method before accepting assignments.

5. *Availability*: Mystery shopping assignments may not always be available, as it depends on the needs of the companies and the availability of other shoppers. Make sure you have alternative sources of income and a flexible schedule if you plan to rely on mystery shopping for passive income.

6. *Reporting Accuracy*: Mystery shopping assignments require accurate and detailed reporting. Make sure you're able to follow the instructions and report your findings accurately.

7. ***Confidentiality***: Mystery shopping assignments may require you to keep the details of the assignment confidential. Make sure you're comfortable with the level of confidentiality required.

8. ***Reputation Management***: Building a positive reputation with mystery shopping companies is important for earning repeat business and referrals. Be reliable, communicative, and respectful of the company's needs.

The amount of money you can make as a mystery shopper can vary widely depending on various factors such as the number of assignments you complete, the type of assignments, and the pay rates offered by the companies you work with. According to data from ***Indeed***, the average pay rate for a mystery shopper in the United States is around $15 per hour, with some companies offering rates ranging from around $10 to $30 per hour. Assuming you complete an average of 10 assignments per week, you could potentially earn around $600 to $1,200 per month as a mystery shopper.

However, it's important to note that the actual amount earned per month as a mystery shopper can vary widely and depends on various factors such as the availability of assignments in your area, your level of experience, and the reputation of the companies you work with. Some mystery shopping assignments may also require additional expenses such as travel costs or purchasing items to evaluate.

Additionally, it's important to carefully evaluate companies and ensure they are legitimate and reputable before accepting mystery shopping assignments, as some companies may be scams or may require payment to access assignments.

Mystery shopping can be a fun and flexible way to earn passive income. However, it's important to be cautious when signing up with mystery shopping companies, as there are scams out there. Be sure to research companies thoroughly before signing up and never pay a fee to become a mystery shopper.

Chapter 9: Emerging Opportunities

NFT Trading

In recent years, the rise of Non-Fungible Tokens (NFTs) has brought a new opportunity for generating passive income. NFTs are unique digital assets that are stored on a blockchain, making them scarce and valuable. One way to make money with NFTs is through NFT trading, where investors buy and sell NFTs on a marketplace for a profit.

NFT trading works similarly to traditional trading, where investors buy low and sell high. NFTs can be anything from digital art, music, videos, or even virtual real estate. When an investor buys an NFT, they own a unique digital asset whose value can appreciate over time. They can then choose to sell the NFT on a marketplace such as *OpenSea* or *Nifty Gateway*, where buyers can bid on the asset. If the value of the NFT has increased since the investor bought it, they can sell it for a profit.

NFT trading has several benefits, including:

1. *Passive Income*: NFT trading can generate passive income as investors can hold onto NFTs and sell them for a profit at a later date.
2. *High Potential Returns*: NFTs value can appreciate quickly, leading to high potential returns on investment.
3. *Diversification*: Investing in NFTs can diversify an investor's portfolio, reducing their overall risk.
4. *Low Barrier to Entry*: Unlike traditional investments, NFT trading has a low barrier to entry, allowing anyone to invest in digital assets.

There are several resources available for NFT trading. Some of the more popular include:

1. *OpenSea* - A popular NFT marketplace where users can buy, sell, and discover NFTs.
2. *Rarible* - Another NFT marketplace where users can buy and sell NFTs, as well as create their own.
3. *SuperRare* - A curated NFT marketplace focused on high-quality digital art.

4. *Nifty Gateway* - A marketplace for buying, selling, and minting NFTs with a focus on popular artists and brands.
5. *NBA Top Shot* - A marketplace for officially licensed NBA NFTs, including highlights and moments from games.
6. *Foundation* - An invitation-only NFT marketplace for high-quality digital art and collectibles.
7. *CryptoKitties* - A popular NFT game where users can buy, sell, and breed virtual cats.
8. *Binance* NFT - An NFT marketplace from the popular cryptocurrency exchange Binance.
9. *Mintable* - A platform for creating and selling NFTs with customizable features and royalties.
10. *KnownOrigin* - A curated NFT marketplace focused on digital art, with a strong emphasis on the artist community.

If you're considering NFT trading for passive income, here are some things to be aware of:

1. *Volatility*: NFT trading is a highly volatile market, with prices fluctuating rapidly. Be aware of the risks involved and only invest what you can afford to lose.
2. *Knowledge*: It's important to have a good understanding of the NFT market and the specific NFTs you're interested in trading. Do your research and stay informed on market trends and news.
3. *Platform Fees*: NFT trading platforms may charge fees for transactions, so be aware of these fees and factor them into your earnings.
4. *Authenticity*: Authenticity is important in the NFT market, as there have been cases of fraudulent NFTs. Make sure you're purchasing NFTs from reputable sources and that they have been verified as authentic.
5. *Liquidity*: NFTs can be illiquid, meaning that it may be difficult to sell them quickly. Be prepared to hold onto your NFTs for a while, if necessary.
6. *Taxes*: NFT trading may have tax implications, so be aware of the tax laws in your country and keep accurate records of your transactions.

7. ***Reputation Management***: Building a positive reputation in the NFT trading community is important for earning repeat business and referrals. Be reliable, communicative, and respectful of other traders.

Assuming you have some knowledge of the NFT market and can identify valuable NFTs to buy and sell, you could potentially earn a significant amount of money each month. However, the actual amount earned can vary widely and is dependent on the market conditions and the demand for the specific NFTs you are trading.

It's important to note that NFT trading can also be risky, as the value of NFTs can fluctuate rapidly and there is no guarantee of making a profit. Additionally, NFT trading requires a certain level of knowledge and expertise, as well as access to the necessary tools and platforms for buying and selling NFTs.

NFT trading is an emerging opportunity for generating passive income. As the market for NFTs continues to grow, investors can benefit from diversifying their portfolio with unique digital assets. With a low barrier to entry and the potential for high returns, NFT trading is an attractive option for those looking to make passive income in the digital age. As always, it's important to do your own research and carefully consider the risks and potential rewards before investing in any new opportunity.

Crypto Staking

In recent years, cryptocurrencies have gained significant popularity as an investment option. One way to earn passive income through cryptocurrency is through crypto staking. In this chapter, we will discuss what crypto staking is, how it works, and how it can generate passive income.

Crypto staking is the process of holding a certain amount of cryptocurrency in a digital wallet for a specific period and earning rewards for it. It is a consensus mechanism used to validate transactions on a blockchain network, and staking enables users to participate in this validation process. In other words, crypto staking involves locking up a certain amount of cryptocurrency in a wallet for a specific period to support the network and earn rewards for doing so.

Crypto staking is a relatively simple process. Users need to hold a certain amount of cryptocurrency in a staking wallet, which is connected to a blockchain network that supports staking. By holding their cryptocurrency in the staking wallet, users become validators for that particular blockchain network, and they earn rewards for validating transactions.

The rewards for staking cryptocurrency can vary, depending on the network and the amount of cryptocurrency staked. In some cases, the rewards can be as high as 10% or more per year. The staking period can also vary, from a few days to several months or even years.

Crypto staking can be a good source of passive income for several reasons. First, it is relatively easy to get started with staking. Users can stake their cryptocurrency through staking wallets, which are often provided by the blockchain network. Additionally, staking does not require any specialized knowledge or hardware, unlike mining.

Second, staking rewards are often higher than other forms of passive income, such as traditional savings accounts or bonds. This is because the rewards are directly tied to the performance of the blockchain network and can vary based on demand.

Third, staking allows users to earn passive income while also supporting the blockchain network. By staking their cryptocurrency, users contribute to the security and decentralization of the network.

There are many blockchain networks that support staking, and each network has its staking process and requirements. Here are some popular blockchain networks that support staking:

1. *Ethereum*: Ethereum is a decentralized blockchain platform that allows for the creation of smart contracts and decentralized applications.
2. *Cardano*: Cardano is a blockchain platform that aims to provide a more secure and scalable infrastructure for decentralized applications.
3. *Polkadot*: Polkadot is a next-generation blockchain protocol that allows for interoperability between different blockchains.
4. *Cosmos*: Cosmos is a decentralized network of independent blockchains that can communicate with each other through the Inter-Blockchain Communication protocol.
5. *Tezos*: Tezos is a self-amending blockchain platform that allows for the creation and deployment of smart contracts and decentralized applications.

To get started with crypto staking, users need to choose a blockchain network that supports staking and then select a staking wallet that is compatible with that network. Some popular staking wallets include:

1. *MyEtherWallet* (MEW): MyEtherWallet (MEW) is a free, open-source, client-side interface that allows users to generate, store, and manage Ethereum and Ethereum-based tokens securely.
2. *Ledger Live*: Ledger Live is a desktop and mobile app that enables users to manage their cryptocurrency assets and interact with multiple blockchains, with an emphasis on security.
3. *Trust Wallet*: Trust Wallet is a mobile wallet for Android and iOS devices that provides users with a secure and intuitive way to store, manage, and trade cryptocurrencies.

4. ***Atomic Wallet***: Atomic Wallet is a decentralized, non-custodial wallet that allows users to manage over 500 cryptocurrencies and exchange them instantly through built-in atomic swaps.

Users should research the staking requirements and rewards for each blockchain network before choosing one to stake their cryptocurrency. Additionally, users should consider the risks associated with staking, such as the possibility of losing their staked cryptocurrency if the network is compromised or if they fail to meet the staking requirements.

The amount of money you can make from crypto staking can vary widely depending on various factors such as the cryptocurrency you stake, the staking reward percentage, the duration of the staking period, and the market conditions.

Assuming you stake a popular cryptocurrency such as Ethereum, which currently offers a staking reward of around 5-6% annually and stake a significant amount of the cryptocurrency for a full year, you could potentially earn several hundred to several thousand dollars per month, depending on the amount staked and the current market value of the cryptocurrency.

However, it's important to note that the actual amount earned from crypto staking can vary widely and is dependent on various factors such as the staking reward percentage, the volatility of the cryptocurrency market, and the risks associated with the specific cryptocurrency being staked.

Additionally, it's important to carefully research and evaluate the platform or wallet used for staking, as some platforms may charge fees or may not be reputable or secure.

Crypto staking is an emerging opportunity for passive income that can be a good investment option for those interested in the cryptocurrency market. However, users should conduct thorough research and understand the risks associated with staking before investing their cryptocurrency.

Cryptocurrency Mining

Cryptocurrency mining is a process by which new digital coins are created and transactions are verified in a decentralized network. This chapter will explore how cryptocurrency mining can generate passive income, the different types of mining, the equipment needed, and the risks involved.

There are two types of cryptocurrency mining: solo mining and pool mining. Solo mining involves the miner competing with other miners to solve complex mathematical equations to validate a transaction and earn the cryptocurrency reward. Pool mining involves multiple miners pooling their resources to solve the mathematical equations and share the reward.

To start mining, a miner needs a computer with a powerful graphics processing unit (GPU) or application-specific integrated circuit (ASIC) and a software program designed for mining. Other necessary equipment includes a mining rig, power supply unit (PSU), cooling system, and internet connection.

There are several things to consider when it comes to cryptocurrency mining as a passive income opportunity:

1. *Initial investment*: Cryptocurrency mining requires a significant initial investment in hardware and software.
2. *Energy costs*: Mining cryptocurrency requires a lot of energy, and the cost of electricity can vary greatly depending on your location.
3. *Mining difficulty*: The difficulty of mining cryptocurrencies can increase over time, which can impact the profitability of your mining operation.
4. *Market volatility*: The value of cryptocurrencies can be highly volatile, which can impact the profitability of your mining operation.
5. *Technical knowledge*: Mining cryptocurrency requires technical knowledge, and it can be challenging for beginners to get started.
6. *Maintenance and* upkeep: Mining equipment requires regular maintenance and upkeep to keep it running smoothly.

7. **Regulatory environment**: The regulatory environment for cryptocurrencies and mining can vary greatly depending on your location, so it's important to stay informed about any changes or developments.

There are several free resources available for cryptocurrency mining, including mining software such as **CGMiner**, **EasyMiner**, and **Claymore's Dual Miner**. Mining pool websites like **Slush Pool**, **F2Pool**, and **Poolin** offer free account creation and low fees. Online forums such as **BitcoinTalk** and **Reddit** also provide valuable information and insights into mining.

If you're considering cryptocurrency mining for passive income, here are some things to be aware of:

1. **Costs**: Cryptocurrency mining requires specialized equipment and energy consumption, which can be expensive. Be aware of the costs involved and factor them into your earnings.
2. **Difficulty**: Cryptocurrency mining is becoming increasingly difficult as more miners enter the market. It may be more challenging to earn a profit from mining as the difficulty increases.
3. **Rewards**: Cryptocurrency mining rewards may fluctuate depending on the market value of the cryptocurrency being mined. Be aware of the volatility of cryptocurrency prices and the potential impact on your earnings.
4. **Technical knowledge**: Cryptocurrency mining requires technical knowledge and experience with computer hardware and software. Make sure you have the necessary knowledge or are willing to learn before investing in mining equipment.
5. **Maintenance**: Cryptocurrency mining equipment requires regular maintenance and upgrades to ensure optimal performance. Be prepared to invest time and resources into maintaining your mining equipment.
6. **Regulatory environment**: Cryptocurrency mining may be subject to regulatory restrictions in some jurisdictions. Be aware of the regulatory environment in your country and any potential legal implications.

The amount of money you can make from cryptocurrency mining can vary widely depending on various factors such as the cryptocurrency being mined, the difficulty level of the mining process, the cost of electricity, and the type of mining hardware used.

Cryptocurrency mining involves using specialized hardware to solve complex mathematical problems and validate transactions on the network, earning rewards in the form of newly minted cryptocurrency.

Assuming you have access to powerful mining hardware and cheap electricity, you could potentially earn several hundred to several thousand dollars per month mining popular cryptocurrencies such as Bitcoin or Ethereum. However, it's important to note that the actual amount earned can vary widely and is dependent on various factors such as the current market value of the cryptocurrency being mined and the level of competition in the mining process.

It's also important to note that cryptocurrency mining can be costly and time-consuming, as it requires significant investments in hardware and electricity, and involves constant monitoring and maintenance of the mining equipment.

Cryptocurrency mining can be a lucrative source of passive income, but it requires a significant investment in equipment and electricity costs. It is important to research and understand the risks involved and stay up to date on the latest mining technology and trends. With the right resources and knowledge, cryptocurrency mining can be a profitable and rewarding venture.

Virtual Real Estate

Virtual real estate, or the ownership of digital space, is a new and exciting way to earn passive income. In this chapter, we'll explore how virtual real estate works, how to get started, and some of the best resources available.

Virtual real estate refers to digital land, property, or assets that exist only in the virtual world. This includes virtual spaces like *Second Life*, *Decentraland*, and *The Sandbox*, as well as *NFTs* (non-fungible tokens) that represent ownership of digital assets like artwork, music, and more.

Getting started in virtual real estate is relatively easy. First, you need to choose a platform to invest in. Once you've chosen a platform, you can purchase virtual land, buildings, and other assets. You can then develop these assets and earn passive income through rent, advertising, and more. Some of the more popular resources for virtual real estate are:

1. *Decentraland*: Decentraland is a virtual world that is built on the Ethereum blockchain. Users can buy virtual land in the world, build on it, and monetize their creations.
2. *Somnium Space*: Somnium Space is a virtual reality platform where users can buy virtual land, build on it, and monetize their creations.
3. *The Sandbox*: The Sandbox is a virtual world that is built on the blockchain. Users can buy virtual land in the world, build on it, and monetize their creations.
4. *OpenSea*: OpenSea is a marketplace for buying and selling virtual assets, including virtual real estate.
5. *VRChat*: VRChat is a virtual reality platform where users can create and share their own virtual experiences, including virtual real estate.
6. *Cryptovoxels*: Cryptovoxels is a virtual world that is built on the Ethereum blockchain. Users can buy virtual land in the world, build on it, and monetize their creations.
7. *High Fidelity*: High Fidelity is a virtual reality platform that allows users to create and share their own virtual experiences, including virtual real estate.

8. *Second Life*: Second Life is a virtual world where users can create and monetize their own virtual content, including virtual real estate.

9. *Axie Infinity*: Axie Infinity is a blockchain-based game where players can earn cryptocurrency by playing the game and collecting rare digital creatures.

10. *SuperWorld*: SuperWorld is a virtual world that is built on the blockchain. Users can buy virtual land in the world, build on it, and monetize their creations.

11. *Nifty Gateway*: Nifty Gateway is a marketplace for NFTs, which can represent ownership of digital assets like artwork, music, and more. You can purchase and sell NFTs to earn passive income.

If you're considering investing in virtual real estate for passive income, here are some things to be aware of:

1. *Market volatility*: Virtual real estate, like any other investment, can be subject to market fluctuations. Be aware of the risks involved and only invest what you can afford to lose.

2. *Platform fees*: Virtual real estate platforms may charge fees for transactions and maintenance of virtual properties. Be aware of these fees and factor them into your earnings.

3. *Authenticity*: Authenticity is important in virtual real estate, as there have been cases of fraudulent virtual properties. Make sure you're investing in virtual real estate from reputable sources and that they have been verified as authentic.

4. *Platform stability*: The stability and security of the virtual real estate platform you choose is important to consider. Look for platforms that have a good reputation for security and uptime.

5. *User adoption*: Virtual real estate is dependent on user adoption and activity. Be sure to invest in a virtual real estate platform that has a thriving community and activity levels.

6. *Revenue streams*: Virtual real estate can generate passive income through renting or leasing out properties, advertising, or other revenue streams. Consider the revenue streams available on the platform you're investing in and the potential earnings.

7. ***Regulation***: The regulation of virtual real estate may vary depending on the platform and jurisdiction. Be aware of the regulatory environment in your country and any potential legal implications.

The amount of money you can make from virtual real estate can vary widely depending on various factors such as the platform or game used, the demand for virtual real estate within that platform or game, and the rarity or uniqueness of the virtual property being sold.

Within platforms like ***Decentraland***, ***The Sandbox***, and ***Second Life***, virtual land parcels and buildings can sell for anywhere from a few hundred dollars to several thousand dollars or more, depending on the location and other factors such as the size and level of development.

Assuming you invest in virtual real estate within a popular platform and are able to acquire and sell virtual properties at a profit, you could potentially earn several hundred to several thousand dollars per month or more. However, it's important to note that the actual amount earned can vary widely and is dependent on various factors such as the demand and market conditions within the specific platform or game.

Virtual real estate is a new and exciting way to earn passive income in the digital world. By investing in virtual land, buildings, and other assets, you can develop and monetize your properties to earn income through a variety of means. With the right platform and strategy, virtual real estate can be a lucrative and rewarding investment opportunity.

Decentralized finance (DeFi)

Decentralized Finance (DeFi) refers to financial applications built on blockchain technology that operate without intermediaries like banks. DeFi provides a platform for individuals to participate in financial transactions, investments, and lending without relying on centralized authorities. This chapter will explore how DeFi can generate passive income and provide free resources for those interested in getting started.

DeFi applications operate on blockchain technology and are designed to provide access to traditional financial services without intermediaries. These services include cryptocurrency trading, lending, borrowing, and investing. DeFi is an emerging opportunity for investors to generate passive income by participating in these financial activities and earning rewards in the form of interest or yield.

There are several ways to generate passive income through DeFi. One way is by lending cryptocurrency to others through lending platforms like *Compound* or *Aave*. Lenders earn interest on the loans they provide, and this interest can be reinvested to generate more passive income.

Another way to generate passive income is by providing liquidity to decentralized exchanges like Uniswap. Liquidity providers earn a share of the trading fees generated by the platform, providing a passive income stream. Additionally, investors can earn passive income through yield farming, which involves staking cryptocurrency in liquidity pools to earn rewards.

Getting started with DeFi can be daunting, but there are several free resources available to help. Websites like *DeFi Pulse* and *DeFi Prime* provide a comprehensive overview of different DeFi applications, including lending platforms, decentralized exchanges, and yield farming protocols. These sites also provide information on the risks associated with DeFi investments.

For those looking to invest in DeFi, several wallets, including *MetaMask* and *Trust Wallet*, provide easy access to DeFi applications. Additionally, there are several DeFi-focused communities on social media platforms like Twitter and Reddit, providing information, insights, and support for new investors.

The amount of money you can make with DeFi can vary widely depending on various factors such as the specific DeFi protocol or application used, the amount of capital invested, and the level of risk taken.

Some popular DeFi applications include decentralized exchanges, yield farming platforms, and lending protocols. Within these applications, users can earn income in the form of interest, trading fees, or rewards for providing liquidity or participating in governance.

Assuming you invest in a popular DeFi protocol and can earn income through interest, fees, or rewards, you could potentially earn several hundred to several thousand dollars per month or more. However, it's important to note that DeFi investments can be highly risky, and the actual amount earned can vary widely depending on various factors such as the volatility of the underlying assets and the level of competition in the DeFi market.

Decentralized Finance (DeFi) is an emerging opportunity for generating passive income through lending, staking, and providing liquidity. As with any investment, it is essential to understand the risks associated with DeFi before investing. However, with the free resources available, investors can educate themselves and start earning passive income through this exciting new financial technology.

Chapter 10: Miscellaneous Passive Income Ideas

Car Advertising

Car advertising, also known as "car wrapping," is a unique way to generate passive income by turning your vehicle into a mobile billboard. Companies pay car owners to wrap their cars with ads, turning their daily commutes into an opportunity to earn money. This chapter will explore how car advertising works, the benefits and drawbacks, and the resources you need to get started.

Car advertising involves wrapping your car with vinyl decals or a full wrap, displaying ads for companies. The company pays car owners a monthly fee to display the ads, and the car owner agrees to drive a certain number of miles per month. The more miles you drive, the more money you can earn.

Car advertising is a unique way to earn passive income. It requires little effort on your part, and you can earn money while driving your car as you normally would. Additionally, the vinyl decals protect your car's paint, and they can be easily removed without damaging the car's surface.

One drawback of car advertising is that it may affect the resale value of your car. Some buyers may not want a car with ads on it. Additionally, you may have to drive a certain number of miles per month to maintain the agreement, which could be inconvenient if you don't drive often. Lastly, some homeowners' associations have rules against wrapped vehicles, so you may want to consult HOA regulations should you live in one.

There are several websites and companies that facilitate car advertising programs. Car owners can sign up with these companies and wait for offers to come in. Here are some resources for finding opportunities:

1. *Wrapify*: Wrapify is a popular car advertising company that connects drivers with brands that want to advertise on their cars. You can sign up to become a driver on their website, and they will match you with brands that fit your driving habits.
2. *Carvertise*: Carvertise is another popular car advertising company that pays drivers to wrap their cars with ads. They have a simple

application process, and once you are accepted, they will send you an advertising campaign that fits your driving habits.

3. ***Free Car Media***: Free Car Media is a car advertising company that pays drivers to put ads on their cars. They work with a variety of companies, from small businesses to large corporations, to find the perfect advertising campaign for your car.

4. ***ReferralCars***: ReferralCars is a car advertising company that pays drivers to refer people to their company. You can sign up to become a driver on their website, and they will send you advertising campaigns that you can share with your friends and family.

5. ***Craigslist***: You can also search for car advertising opportunities on Craigslist. Look for ads that say "get paid to drive your car" or "car advertising opportunities available" to find potential opportunities.

On average, individuals can earn anywhere from $100 to $400 per month for displaying advertisements on their cars. However, some car advertising companies may offer higher payouts for larger and more prominent ads or for longer advertising campaigns.

Remember to always read the terms and conditions carefully before signing up for any car advertising program. Make sure you understand the requirements, compensation, and any potential risks involved. While there are some drawbacks, the benefits of car advertising make it a worthwhile consideration for those looking to earn passive income.

Creating and Selling Stock Footage or Video Clips

In today's digital age, the demand for high-quality video content is increasing day by day. This has opened a new avenue for creative individuals to generate passive income by creating and selling stock footage or video clips. In this chapter, we will explore how you can get started with this lucrative passive income opportunity and some free resources to help you along the way.

To start generating passive income from stock footage and video clips, you can shoot footage of various subjects and locations, such as nature, urban areas, people, and animals. You can also specialize in a particular niche or style, such as aerial footage, time-lapse, or slow motion.

When getting started, here's a checklist of things to consider:

1. *Identify your niche*: Before you start creating stock footage or video clips, it's essential to identify your niche. This can be anything from landscapes and nature to lifestyle and business footage. It's crucial to choose a niche that you are passionate about and have the necessary skills to create compelling footage.

2. *Invest in quality equipment*: To create high-quality stock footage or video clips, you need to invest in good equipment. A good camera, tripod, and lighting equipment are essential to produce professional-looking footage.

3. *Plan and storyboard*: Planning and storyboarding are essential to ensure that your footage tells a story and is useful for potential buyers. Creating a shot list and having a clear idea of what you want to capture can save you time and ensure that your footage is of high quality.

4. *Shoot and edit*: Once you have planned and storyboarded your footage, it's time to start shooting. Make sure you capture your footage in the highest quality possible and edit it to perfection.

5. *Upload and sell*: After editing your footage, upload it to stock footage websites and start selling. Make sure you read the terms

and conditions of each website and price your footage accordingly. Shutterstock, Adobe Stock, Pond5, Storyblocks, and iStock are popular and reputable platforms to consider.

To increase your chances of selling your footage, you should focus on creating high-quality content that meets the needs of your target audience. You should also ensure that your footage is properly tagged with relevant keywords, descriptions, and categories to make it more discoverable in search results. Additionally, promoting your work on social media and other online platforms can help attract potential customers and increase your visibility in the industry.

The amount of money you can earn through selling stock footage or video clips varies depending on the quality of your content, the demand for your subject matter, the number of clips you have available for sale, and the platform you are selling on.

On popular stock footage and video clip marketplaces like *Shutterstock*, *Adobe Stock*, and *Pond5*, contributors can earn anywhere from $0.25 to $5.00 per download, depending on the resolution and license type of the clip. With a large portfolio of high-quality clips, it is possible to earn several hundred dollars or more per month from these marketplaces. Additionally, some stock footage and video clip marketplaces offer revenue-sharing programs for contributors, which can allow you to earn a percentage of the sales revenue generated by your clips over time.

Creating and selling stock footage or video clips can be an excellent source of passive income for creative individuals. By identifying your niche, investing in quality equipment, planning, and storyboarding, shooting & editing, and uploading and selling your footage on stock footage websites, you can earn a steady stream of passive income.

Investing In a Business That Generates Royalties

Investing in a business that generates royalties can be a lucrative source of passive income. Royalties are payments made to the owner of a copyrighted work, such as a book, song, or invention, in exchange for the right to use or sell that work. By investing in a business that owns the copyright to a popular product or service, investors can earn a portion of the revenue generated from the use or sale of that product or service.

For example, a business that owns the copyright to a popular song can earn royalties every time that song is played on the radio or streamed online. Investors who own a share of that business can earn a portion of those royalties without having to be involved in the day-to-day operations of the business.

There are a variety of resources available for individuals looking to invest in businesses that generate royalties. Here are a few:

1. *Royalty Exchange*: Royalty Exchange is an online platform that allows investors to buy and sell royalties from a variety of assets, including music, art, patents, and more. *Royalty Flow*, and *Vindicia* are two more to consider.
2. *The Royalty Exchange Investment Program*: The Royalty Exchange Investment Program is a managed investment service that offers investors access to a diversified portfolio of royalties.
3. *SEC Filings*: Investors can also research businesses that generate royalties by reviewing their SEC filings, which provide information about the company's financials and operations.
4. *Business Brokers*: Business brokers can help investors find businesses that generate royalties that are available for sale.
5. *Industry Associations*: Industry associations, such as the Music Publishers Association, can provide information about businesses that generate royalties in their respective industries.
6. *Financial Advisors*: Investors can also work with financial advisors who specialize in alternative investments, such as

royalties, to help them identify and invest in businesses that generate passive income through royalties.

7. ***Individual Copyrights***: It is also possible to invest in individual copyrights through websites such as ***SongVest*** or ***The Rights Company***.

The amount of money you can make by investing in a business that generates royalties depends on several factors, including the size and profitability of the business, the percentage of royalties you receive, and the terms of the agreement between the business owner and investors.

Royalty payments are typically calculated as a percentage of the revenue generated by the business, so the amount you can earn will depend on the success of the business. In some cases, royalty payments may be fixed and based on a set amount per unit sold or licensed.

For example, if you invest in a business that generates $10,000 per month in royalties and you receive a 10% share, you could earn $1,000 per month in passive income. However, if the business experiences a downturn or there is a decrease in demand for its products or services, your royalty payments may decrease or even stop altogether.

Investing in a business that generates royalties can be a great passive income stream to consider because the investor does not have to actively participate in the business or manage the copyright. However, it is important to thoroughly research the business and its copyrights before investing to ensure that the business has a track record of generating consistent royalties and that the copyright is properly registered and protected.

Subscription Box Services

Subscription box services have become increasingly popular in recent years as a way for people to receive a curated selection of products delivered to their doorstep on a regular basis. As a passive income stream, investing in a subscription box service involves creating a unique concept and partnering with suppliers to offer a selection of products to subscribers on a monthly or quarterly basis.

The first step in creating a successful subscription box service is to develop a unique concept that appeals to a specific target market. Conducting thorough market research will help to identify what products and themes are currently popular, as well as identify any gaps in the market that can be filled by your subscription box service.

Once the concept is established, the next step is to partner with suppliers and select the products that will be included in the subscription box. The products should align with the theme and target market of the subscription box and should be sourced at a price point that allows for a profitable margin.

A website will need to be created to showcase the subscription box service and allow customers to sign up for a subscription. Marketing efforts should focus on reaching the target market through social media, influencer partnerships, and other channels.

Once subscribers have signed up for the service, it will be important to have an efficient system in place for fulfillment and shipping. This may involve outsourcing to a third-party fulfillment center or managing fulfillment in-house.

There are many free resources available for creating a subscription box service. A few of which are:

1. *Launch 27*: A platform that helps entrepreneurs create and launch subscription box services by providing website templates, payment processing, and fulfillment management tools.

2. *Cratejoy*: A marketplace for subscription box services that provides resources for creating and marketing a subscription box service, as well as a platform for managing subscriptions and fulfillment.

3. *Subbly*: Subbly is another subscription box platform that provides everything you need to launch and run a successful subscription business, including customizable website templates, payment processing, and marketing tools.

4. *Mysubscriptionaddiction*: Mysubscriptionaddiction is a website that reviews and curates subscription boxes in various categories, including beauty, food, and lifestyle. By subscribing to their newsletter or following them on social media, you can stay up-to-date on the latest subscription box trends and get ideas for your own subscription box service.

5. *Reddit*: The subreddit *r/SubscriptionBoxes* is a community of subscription box enthusiasts and entrepreneurs where you can connect with others in the industry, ask for advice, and get feedback on your subscription box service.

6. *Google Analytics*: Google Analytics is a free web analytics tool that can help you track your website traffic, monitor user behavior, and gain insights into how your subscription box service is performing.

7. *Canva*: Canva is a free graphic design tool that can help you create eye-catching designs for your subscription box packaging, marketing materials, and social media posts.

8. *Hootsuite*: Hootsuite is a social media management tool that can help you schedule and automate your social media posts, track engagement, and analyze your social media performance.

If you're considering starting a subscription box service for passive income, here are some things to be aware of:

1. *Startup costs*: Starting a subscription box service requires initial investment in product development, marketing, and fulfillment. Be aware of the startup costs involved and plan accordingly.

2. *Customer retention*: The success of your subscription box service depends on customer retention. Make sure you're delivering

quality products and a positive customer experience to retain subscribers.

3. ***Competition***: The subscription box market is competitive, and there may be other similar services targeting the same niche. Be aware of the competition and find ways to differentiate your service and add value.

4. ***Shipping and logistics***: Shipping and logistics can be challenging for subscription box services, particularly as your subscriber base grows. Be sure to have a solid fulfillment process in place to avoid delays or errors.

5. ***Product sourcing***: Sourcing products for your subscription box service can be time-consuming and may require negotiation with suppliers. Be sure to have a plan for sourcing and procuring products.

6. ***Revenue streams***: Subscription box services can generate revenue through subscription fees, advertising, and other revenue streams. Consider the revenue streams available and the potential earnings.

7. ***Regulation***: Subscription box services may be subject to regulation in some jurisdictions, particularly if they involve food, beauty products, or other regulated items. Be aware of the regulatory environment in your country and any potential legal implications.

It's difficult to provide an exact figure for the average monthly income from subscription box services as it varies widely depending on the individual's business model, product offerings, and marketing efforts. However, according to a survey conducted by ***McKinsey & Company***, the average subscription box customer spends about $32 per month on boxes, and the average subscriber is signed up to three boxes at any given time.

Based on this data, an average subscription box business with 1,000 subscribers could potentially generate around $96,000 in monthly revenue. However, it's important to keep in mind that this is just an estimate and that actual earnings may be higher or lower depending on various factors such as the cost of the products included in the box, shipping and handling costs, and marketing expenses. Successful subscription box businesses usually rely on creating a loyal customer base, keeping costs under control, and consistently delivering a high-quality product to their subscribers.

Investing in a subscription box service can provide a source of passive income through recurring monthly or quarterly subscription payments. With the right concept, product selection, and marketing efforts, a successful subscription box service can generate significant revenue and be a rewarding business venture.

Investing in Art

Investing in art can be a lucrative way to generate passive income. Art has long been considered a valuable and collectible asset, with many pieces appreciating in value over time. By investing in art, you can potentially earn a return on your investment through resale or rental income.

One way to invest in art is to purchase works from emerging artists. These artists may not yet have a well-established reputation, but their work may hold value in the future as their career and profile grow. Another option is to purchase works from established artists, which may come with a higher price tag but also potentially offer a greater return on investment.

There are several resources available to find emerging artists to invest in. Here are a few:

1. *Art fairs and exhibitions*: Attending art fairs and exhibitions can be a great way to discover emerging artists. These events often feature a mix of established and up-and-coming artists and provide an opportunity to see their work in person.
2. *Online marketplaces*: Online marketplaces such as *Saatchi Art*, *Artsy*, and *Artfinder* feature a wide range of artists, including many emerging ones. These platforms often offer tools to filter and search for specific types of artwork or artists based on your interests.
3. *Art schools and graduate programs*: Many emerging artists are recent graduates of art schools and graduate programs. By attending student shows or following the alumni network of a particular institution, you can find talented artists who are just starting their careers.
4. *Social media*: Social media platforms such as *Instagram*, *Twitter*, and *Facebook* can be valuable resources for discovering emerging artists. Many artists use these platforms to share their work and build a following, and by following specific hashtags or accounts, you can discover new talent.
5. *Art galleries*: Art galleries often represent emerging artists and can be a valuable resource for discovering new talent. By attending

gallery exhibitions and shows, you can get a sense of the type of artists a particular gallery represents and discover new talent in the process.

When investing in art, it's important to do your research and consider factors such as an artist's career trajectory, exhibition history, and market demand. Working with a reputable art advisor or dealer can also provide valuable insights and guidance in building a successful art portfolio for passive income.

Another way to invest in art is through art funds or exchange-traded funds (ETFs). These funds allow you to invest in a diversified portfolio of artworks, which can help mitigate the risk of investing in a single piece. Art funds may also provide access to works that are not available on the open market.

If you're interested in generating passive income from art, you can consider renting out your collection to museums, galleries, or private collectors. This can provide a steady stream of income without having to sell your artwork.

Finally, you can also consider investing in art-related businesses, such as art storage facilities or art transport companies. These businesses may provide stable returns through their operations and the services they provide to the art industry.

If you're considering investing in art for passive income, here are some things to be aware of:

1. *Market volatility*: The art market can be subject to fluctuations, so be aware of the risks involved and only invest what you can afford to lose.
2. *Authenticity*: Authenticity is crucial in art investment. Be sure to invest in works from reputable artists and reputable sources.
3. *Condition*: The condition of the artwork can impact its value. Be aware of the condition of the artwork before investing.
4. *Artist reputation*: The reputation of the artist can impact the value of the artwork. Consider investing in works by established artists with a proven track record.

5. *Market trends*: Be aware of current and future market trends in the art world, as these can impact the value of your investment.
6. *Storage and insurance*: Proper storage and insurance are crucial for protecting your investment. Be sure to store your artwork in a secure location and insure it against damage or loss.
7. *Taxes*: Taxes can impact the return on your investment. Be aware of tax implications and consult with a tax professional if necessary.

It's difficult to provide an exact figure for the average monthly income from investing in art as it can vary widely depending on the individual's investment strategy, the type and quality of art being invested in, and the overall state of the art market.

However, according to the *2021 Art Market* Report published by *Art Basel* and *UBS*, the global art market saw a 5% increase in sales in 2020 despite the challenges presented by the COVID-19 pandemic. The report states that the top 1% of art sales in 2020 generated more than 63% of the total sales value, indicating that the high-end art market is where most of the earnings are concentrated.

Additionally, art investment returns can vary widely over time, with some works of art appreciating significantly in value while others may decline in value or remain stagnant. Therefore, investing in art requires a significant amount of knowledge and expertise, and it is generally considered to be a long-term investment strategy.

Investing in art can be a viable way to generate passive income. However, as with any investment, it's important to do your research and work with reputable professionals to make informed decisions.

Investing in Wine

Investing in wine can generate passive income through buying and holding quality bottles of wine that increase in value over time. Wine is a tangible asset that can be held for appreciation or sold for profit. The value of wine is determined by factors such as rarity, age, condition, and provenance.

One way to invest in wine is to purchase individual bottles or cases from established wine merchants or auction houses. These merchants often have access to exclusive wines and can provide guidance on investment-grade wines. It is important to do research and seek expert advice before making any investment in wine.

Investing in wine requires patience and a long-term perspective, as wine can take years to mature in taste and appreciate in value. Proper storage and handling of wine is also critical, as temperature fluctuations and exposure to light can damage the wine and reduce its value.

There are several resources to find wine to invest in, including:

1. Wine investment companies: There are several wine investment companies that specialize in acquiring and managing wine collections on behalf of investors. Some examples include *Vinovest*, *Cult Wines*, and *Wine Owners*.
2. Wine auctions: Wine auctions are a great way to find rare and collectible wines. Some of the major auction houses that specialize in wine include *Christie's*, *Sotheby's*, and *Zachys*.
3. Wine merchants: Many wine merchants offer investment-grade wines that are suitable for long-term cellaring. Some of the well-known wine merchants that offer investment-grade wines include *Berry Bros. & Rudd*, *Justerini & Brooks*, and *Corney & Barrow*.
4. Wine clubs: Some wine clubs specialize in offering investment-grade wines to their members. These clubs may offer exclusive access to limited-release wines or pre-arrivals that are not available to the public.

5. Wine publications: Wine publications such as *Wine Spectator* and *Decanter* regularly feature articles on investment-grade wines and provide recommendations on which wines are worth investing in.

It's important to do your due diligence when investing in wine and to work with reputable companies and individuals. Wine investment can be a complex and risky venture, so it's crucial to have a clear investment strategy and to understand the factors that can affect wine values, such as vintage, producer, and provenance.

An alternate way to invest in wine is through wine investment funds. These funds allow investors to pool their money together to purchase wine, often with the guidance of professional wine experts. Here are some ways to find wine investment funds:

1. Do your research: Start by researching wine investment funds online. Look for funds that have a good track record of performance and a solid reputation in the industry. Read reviews and ratings from other investors to get an idea of how successful the fund has been.
2. Consult with a financial advisor: Consider consulting with a financial advisor who specializes in wine investing. They can help you identify reputable funds and provide guidance on which ones may be best suited for your investment goals and risk tolerance.
3. Attend wine investment events: Look for wine investment events in your area or online where you can meet fund managers and other investors. These events are a great way to network and learn more about the industry.
4. Join wine investment groups: Join online communities or social media groups focused on wine investing. These groups can provide valuable insights and tips on investing in wine and can also help you find reputable investment funds.
5. Contact wine merchants: Some wine merchants may also offer investment opportunities or have connections with investment funds. Contact wine merchants in your area to see if they have any recommendations or can provide more information on investing in wine.

Investing in wine can be a lucrative investment strategy, but the amount of money one can make largely depends on several factors such as the quality and rarity of the wine, the overall state of the wine market, and the timing of the investment.

According to some experts, a well-selected wine investment portfolio can potentially generate returns of 10-15% per year, though this can vary widely depending on the individual investments. Some rare and sought-after wines, such as those from top Bordeaux estates, have been known to increase in value by several hundred percent over a period of several years.

It's important to note that investing in wine requires a significant initial investment, and it is generally considered a long-term investment strategy. Furthermore, investing in wine requires knowledge and expertise in the wine industry, including factors such as vintage quality, market demand, and storage conditions.

Remember to do your due diligence when investing in wine or any other asset class. Consult with professionals, conduct thorough research, and understand the risks involved before making any investment decisions. Investing in wine can be a profitable and enjoyable way to generate passive income, but it requires careful consideration, research, and expert guidance to make informed investment decisions.

Investing in Gold or Silver

Investing in gold and silver can be a smart way to diversify your portfolio and generate passive income. These precious metals have been valued for their rarity and beauty for centuries and have been used as a form of currency for just as long.

One way to invest in gold and silver is to purchase physical bullion, such as coins or bars. This can be done through reputable dealers or online marketplaces. The value of physical bullion will fluctuate based on market demand, but it can be a reliable long-term investment. However, keep in mind that there are costs associated with storing and insuring physical bullion.

Another way to invest in gold and silver is through exchange-traded funds (ETFs). These funds hold a portfolio of gold or silver assets, and the value of the ETF shares will fluctuate based on market demand for the underlying assets. ETFs can be bought and sold like stocks, making them a convenient and liquid investment option.

Investing in mining companies that extract gold and silver from the earth can also be a way to generate passive income. These companies may pay dividends to their shareholders, or their stock value may increase as the demand for gold and silver increases.

Additional options for investing in gold and silver include:

1. Precious metals mutual funds: These are funds that invest in the stocks of companies involved in the production or distribution of precious metals. Investors can buy shares of these funds and gain exposure to the precious metals industry without having to directly invest in physical gold or silver.
2. Futures contracts: These are contracts that allow investors to buy or sell a specified amount of gold or silver at a set price and date in the future. Futures contracts can be traded on commodities exchanges, and they can be used to speculate on the price movements of the metals.

3. Online brokers: Some online brokers offer trading platforms for gold and silver, allowing investors to buy and sell the metals in various forms, such as coins, bars, and ETFs.
4. Numismatic dealers: These are businesses that specialize in rare and collectible coins made of gold or silver. Numismatic coins can be more expensive than bullion coins, but they may also have a higher potential for appreciation over time due to their rarity and historical significance.
5. Refiners: Refiners are companies that process raw gold and silver into bars, coins, and other forms of the metals. Some refiners also offer investment products directly to the public, such as fractional ownership of large bars or coins.

Historically, gold and silver have been viewed as safe-haven investments, meaning they tend to hold their value well during economic uncertainty and inflationary periods. As a result, investors may choose to hold a portion of their portfolio in gold and silver to help mitigate risk and protect against inflation. The price of gold and silver can fluctuate significantly in the short term, but over the long term, it has generally trended upwards. Over the past decade, the price of gold has risen by around 50%, while the price of silver has risen by around 25%.

Gold and silver can be volatile. It is generally considered a long-term investment strategy. Furthermore, the returns on gold and silver investments may not keep pace with the returns on other asset classes such as stocks and real estate. It's important to do your research and understand the risks involved in investing in gold and silver. The value of these precious metals can be volatile and may be affected by factors such as global economic conditions, political instability, and inflation. Working with a financial advisor or investment professional can help you make informed decisions about how to invest in gold and silver to generate passive income.

Investing in a Franchise

Investing in a franchise can generate passive income by allowing individuals to own and operate a business that is already established and has a proven track record of success. Franchising is a popular option for individuals who want to be their own boss but do not have the experience or resources to start a business from scratch.

When you invest in a franchise, you typically pay an initial franchise fee and ongoing royalties in exchange for the right to use the franchisor's brand name, products, and services. The franchisor provides you with training and support, as well as a proven business model, marketing materials, and other resources to help you succeed.

Franchise opportunities are available in a wide range of industries, including food and beverage, retail, health & wellness, automotive, and many more. Some popular franchises include *McDonald's*, *Subway*, *7-Eleven*, and *Anytime Fitness*.

To invest in a franchise, it is important to do your research and choose a reputable franchisor with a proven track record of success. You should also carefully review the franchise agreement and financial disclosures to ensure that you understand the costs and obligations associated with owning and operating a franchise.

In addition to the initial investment, you should also consider the ongoing costs and time commitment required to run a franchise. While owning a franchise can generate passive income, it is not completely hands-off, and you will need to be involved in managing the day-to-day operations of your business. There are several resources available to help you find the right franchise to invest in. Here are some of the most useful ones:

1. *Franchise expos*: Attend franchise expos to meet with franchisors and learn more about their businesses. These expos are usually held in major cities and provide a great opportunity to network with other investors.

2. *Franchise directories*: Franchise directories list hundreds of franchises in different industries, allowing you to narrow down your search based on your interests and budget.
3. *Franchise consultants*: Franchise consultants can help you navigate the world of franchising and provide guidance on the best franchises to invest in based on your goals and budget.
4. *Online resources*: There are several websites dedicated to helping people find and invest in franchises. Some popular options include *Franchise.com*, *Franchise Direct*, and *Franchise Gator*.
5. *Industry associations*: Joining industry associations related to the franchise you are interested in can help you gain valuable insights and connect with other franchise owners. Some examples include the *International Franchise Association* (IFA) and the *Franchise Business Network* (FBN).

The amount of money that you can make by investing in a franchise will vary depending on several factors, including the initial investment, the type of franchise, the location, and your ability to manage the business effectively.

Generally, franchisees can expect to earn a return on investment of 10-20% annually, although this can vary greatly depending on the industry and franchise. Some franchises may provide a steady income of a few thousand dollars per month, while others may generate tens of thousands or even hundreds of thousands of dollars per month.

When considering a franchise, it's important to do your due diligence and research the franchisor thoroughly. This includes reviewing their financial statements, talking to other franchisees, and understanding the terms of the franchise agreement. Working with a lawyer or accountant who specializes in franchising can also be helpful in ensuring that you are making a sound investment decision.

Sell Your Unused or Unwanted Items on Online Marketplaces

Selling unused or unwanted items can be a great way to generate passive income. With so many online marketplaces available today, it's easier than ever to sell items you no longer need or want. You can sell anything from clothing and electronics to furniture and household goods.

One popular platform for selling used items is *eBay*. eBay has a massive user base and allows you to sell almost anything you can think of. You can set up an account and list your items for sale, and buyers from all over the world can bid on them or buy them outright. eBay charges a small fee for each item sold, but it's generally worth it for the exposure and ease of use.

Another popular platform for selling used items is *Facebook Marketplace*. Facebook Marketplace is a free platform where you can list your items for sale and connect with buyers in your local area. You can also join local buy and sell groups on Facebook, which can be a great way to connect with buyers and sellers in your area.

In addition to online marketplaces, you can also sell items at local flea markets or garage sales. These options may require more effort on your part, as you'll need to set up a booth or table and spend time haggling with buyers. However, they can be a great way to get rid of many items at once.

When selling items for passive income, it's important to price them appropriately. You want to make sure you're getting a fair price for your items, but you also don't want to price them too high and scare off potential buyers. Do some research on similar items to get an idea of what they've recently sold for, not what they're listed for, and price your items accordingly. Just because something is listed for $10,000 does not mean it is going to sell for $10,000.

An alternative to selling unused items you already own is to source items to flip. There are many places to source items to flip on eBay, and the key is to find items that are in demand and can be sold for a profit. Here are some popular options:

1. Thrift stores: Thrift stores such as **Goodwill** or **Salvation Army** are a great place to find items to flip on eBay, as they often have a wide range of items at low prices. Look for items that are in good condition and have a high resale value, such as vintage clothing, books, and collectibles.

2. Garage sales: Garage sales are another great place to find items to flip on eBay. Look for items that are priced low but have a high resale value, such as electronics, furniture, and toys.

3. Estate sales: Estate sales can be a treasure trove of items to flip on eBay, especially if you're interested in antiques and collectibles. Look for items that are in good condition and have a high resale value, such as jewelry, art, and vintage clothing.

4. Online marketplaces: Online marketplaces like **Facebook Marketplace**, **Craigslist**, and **OfferUp** can be a great source of items to flip on **eBay**. Look for items that are priced low but have a high resale value, such as electronics, furniture, and appliances.

5. Clearance sales: Clearance sales at stores like **Walmart** and **Target** can be a great source of items to flip on eBay, especially if you can find items that are marked down significantly. Look for items that are in demand and have a high resale value, such as electronics, toys, and home goods.

6. Wholesale suppliers: If you're interested in flipping items on eBay on a larger scale, you may want to consider working with a wholesale supplier. Wholesale suppliers can provide you with bulk items at a discounted price, which can be resold on eBay for a profit. However, be sure to do your research and find a reputable supplier.

Here are some of the top online marketplaces you can use to sell your unwanted items:

1. **eBay** - an online auction and shopping website where you can sell various items, both new and used.

2. **Amazon** - an online retailer that allows you to sell your products through their website. You can sell new or used items, as well as handmade products.

3. *Facebook Marketplace* - a platform integrated with Facebook where you can sell items to people in your local area.
4. *Craigslist* - a classified advertisements website where you can sell a variety of items to people in your local area.
5. *Etsy* - an online marketplace for handmade and vintage items, as well as unique factory-manufactured items.
6. *Poshmark* - an online marketplace for new and gently used clothing and accessories.
7. *Mercari* - an online marketplace for new and used items, including clothing, electronics, and home goods.
8. *Decluttr* - an online marketplace for used electronics, books, and media items.
9. *OfferUp* - an online marketplace for buying and selling items locally, including electronics, furniture, and clothing.

According to some estimates, experienced sellers can make a few thousand dollars per month or more selling items on these platforms, while beginners may start out earning a few hundred dollars per month. However, it's important to note that there are also costs associated with selling on these platforms, including fees for listing, shipping, and payment processing, which can impact the overall profitability of the business.

Selling unused or unwanted items can be a great way to generate passive income. It may require some effort on your part, but the payoff can be well worth it. Plus, it can be a great way to declutter your home and simplify your life.

Retail Arbitrage

Retail arbitrage is the practice of buying products from one retail outlet and selling them at a higher price in another location. It involves finding products that are on sale or clearance in one store and reselling them at a profit in another store or online marketplace. This method can generate passive income by taking advantage of price differences between retailers.

Retail arbitrage can be done both in physical stores and online. In physical stores, retail arbitrage involves visiting stores and looking for products that are on clearance or being sold at a discount. The items can be anything from clothing, toys, electronics, and even groceries. Once the items have been purchased, they can be sold on online marketplaces such as *eBay*, *Amazon*, or *Facebook Marketplace*.

Online retail arbitrage involves searching for products online that are being sold at a lower price and reselling them at a higher price on other online marketplaces. For example, an individual may find a product on sale on a retailer's website and resell it on Amazon or eBay at a higher price. This method can be done from the comfort of one's home and can be a great way to generate passive income.

When engaging in retail arbitrage, it's important to consider the costs involved in acquiring the products and selling them. Shipping costs, taxes, and fees associated with selling on online marketplaces should be factored into the selling price. It's also important to consider the potential risks involved, such as the products being damaged during shipping or not selling at the desired price.

There are several resources available for those interested in retail arbitrage, including:

1. *Online marketplaces*: Retail arbitrage typically involves buying products at a low price and then reselling them at a higher price. Online marketplaces like Amazon and eBay are popular sources for finding products to buy and resell.
2. *Retail stores*: Retail arbitrage can also involve buying clearance items or products on sale at retail stores and then reselling them

online for a profit. Popular retail stores for sourcing products include *Walmart, Target,* and *Home Depot.*

3. *Apps and tools*: There are several apps and tools available that can help with retail arbitrage, including price comparison tools like *CamelCamelCamel* and *Keepa,* which track prices and sales histories for products on *Amazon.*

4. *Online communities*: There are many online communities and forums dedicated to retail arbitrage, where sellers can share tips and advice on finding and reselling products. Popular communities include the *Amazon FBA subreddit* and the *Retail Arbitrage Facebook* group.

5. *Courses and training programs*: For those looking to take their retail arbitrage to the next level, there are several courses and training programs available that can teach advanced strategies for finding and reselling profitable products. Some popular programs include *The Wholesale Formula* and *Online Selling Experiment.*

6. *Wholesale suppliers*: Another strategy for retail arbitrage is to source products directly from wholesale suppliers. There are several wholesale directories available, such as *SaleHoo* and *Wholesale Central,* that can connect sellers with reputable suppliers in a variety of product categories.

If you're considering retail arbitrage for passive income, here are some things to be aware of:

1. *Margins*: Retail arbitrage relies on finding products that can be sold at a profit. Be aware of the margins involved and ensure that there is enough profit to justify the effort.

2. *Sourcing*: Sourcing products for retail arbitrage can be time-consuming and may require visiting multiple stores or online marketplaces. Be sure to have a plan for sourcing and procuring products.

3. *Competition*: The retail arbitrage market can be competitive, particularly for popular products. Be aware of the competition and find ways to differentiate your offerings or find niche markets.

4. *Fulfillment*: Fulfillment can be a challenge for retail arbitrage, particularly if you're selling on multiple marketplaces. Be sure to have a solid fulfillment process in place to avoid delays or errors.
5. *Returns and customer service*: Be aware of the returns and customer service policies of the marketplaces you're selling on and be prepared to handle any issues that may arise.
6. *Sales taxes*: Sales taxes can be complex for retail arbitrage, particularly if you're selling across multiple states or countries. Be aware of the sales tax implications and consult with a tax professional if necessary.
7. *Legal issues*: Retail arbitrage can raise legal issues, particularly if you're reselling products that are copyrighted, trademarked, or patented. Be aware of the legal implications and ensure that you're complying with all applicable laws and regulations.

Some experienced sellers have reported earning anywhere from a few hundred dollars to several thousand dollars per month through retail arbitrage. However, it's important to note that success in retail arbitrage requires a lot of hard work, research, and a keen eye for spotting profitable deals. Additionally, there may be some costs involved such as transportation, storage, and listing fees on online marketplaces.

Retail arbitrage can be a profitable way to generate passive income by taking advantage of price differences between retailers. With proper research and consideration of costs and risks, individuals can turn this practice into a successful source of income.

Sell Your Old Textbooks

Selling your old textbooks can be an excellent way to generate passive income. When you're finished with a class, chances are you won't be needing that textbook anymore. Instead of letting it collect dust on your bookshelf, you can turn it into cash.

One way to sell your old textbooks is through online marketplaces such as *Amazon, eBay*, or *BookFinder*. These sites make it easy to list your books and connect with potential buyers. You can set your own prices or use tools such as Amazon's trade-in program to get an instant offer.

Another option is to sell your textbooks directly to college bookstores or other local buyers. Many schools have buyback programs that offer cash or store credit for used books. You can also check with independent bookstores or secondhand shops in your area to see if they buy textbooks.

To get the most money for your textbooks, it's important to keep them in good condition. Avoid highlighting or underlining and protect the covers with a plastic cover. If you have access to the original packaging, that can also increase the value.

You may also want to consider timing your sales to coincide with the beginning of the school year or the start of a new semester. This is when demand for textbooks is highest, and you may be able to command a higher price.

Don't own any textbooks? There are several ways to source cheap textbooks to flip for profit:

1. *Campus bulletin boards*: Many students post ads on campus bulletin boards to sell their old textbooks. Check out bulletin boards on campuses near you to see if you can find any good deals.
2. *Online classifieds*: Online classifieds such as *Craigslist*, *Facebook Marketplace*, and *Kijiji* can be a great resource for finding cheap textbooks. Simply search for "textbooks" in the classifieds section and you'll likely find several listings.

3. ***Thrift stores***: Check out your local thrift stores, such as ***Goodwill*** or ***Salvation Army***, for used textbooks. You may have to do some digging, but you might be able to find some great deals.

4. ***Garage sales***: Keep an eye out for garage sales in your neighborhood, as many people sell their unwanted textbooks at these events.

5. ***Online retailers***: Check out online retailers such as ***Amazon*** or ***Chegg*** for deals on textbooks. Sometimes you can find textbooks at a discount, especially if you buy used or previous editions.

6. ***Book sales***: Keep an eye out for book sales in your area, as they may have textbooks available for purchase at discounted prices.

7. ***Friends and family***: Ask friends and family members if they have any old textbooks they no longer need. They may be willing to sell them to you at a discounted price.

The amount of money the average person can generate monthly selling old textbooks can vary widely depending on factors such as the number of textbooks sold, their condition, the demand for them, and the selling platform used.

On average, individuals can earn around $50-100 per month selling used textbooks, but this can vary greatly based on the factors mentioned. Some sellers may have a steady stream of sales and make a consistent income, while others may only sell textbooks occasionally and generate a more sporadic income. Ultimately, the amount of money a person can make selling old textbooks will depend on their individual circumstances and the effort they put into the process.

Sell Your Unused Gift Cards

Selling unused gift cards can be a great way to generate passive income. If you have a stack of gift cards lying around that you haven't used, you can sell them online and turn them into cash.

One way to sell unused gift cards is through online marketplaces such as *Raise*, *Gift Card Granny*, and *Cardpool*. These platforms allow you to sell your gift cards for cash or trade them for other gift cards. They also provide a guarantee to buyers that the gift card is legitimate and has the stated balance.

Another option is to sell your gift cards on *eBay* or *Amazon*. This can be a good choice if you have a rare or high-value gift card, as you may be able to sell it for more than its face value.

When selling gift cards, it's important to keep in mind that you may not get the full value of the card. Most reselling platforms take a commission, and buyers may not be willing to pay the full value of the card. Additionally, some gift cards may have restrictions or expiration dates that could impact their value.

Some retailers may also offer gift card buyback programs. For example, *Target* and *Walmart* allow you to trade in unwanted gift cards for store credit. *Coinstar Exchange* kiosks are in many grocery stores and allow you to trade in your unwanted gift cards for cash.

To get the most out of selling your unused gift cards, it's important to research the value of your card and compare offers from different reselling platforms. You may also want to consider using the gift card for a purchase and then selling the item instead of selling the gift card directly.

The amount of money an average person can generate monthly by selling unused gift cards can vary greatly depending on the value and popularity of the cards. According to some estimates, you can typically sell a gift card for up to 92% of its value, which means if you have a $100 gift card, you could potentially sell it for $92. However, this amount can vary depending on the platform you use to sell the card, the demand for the specific brand of the gift card, and other factors.

Selling unused gift cards can be a simple and easy way to generate passive income from items you may have otherwise discarded.

Sell Your Plasma

Selling your plasma can be a way to earn some extra cash on the side, as it can generate passive income. Plasma is the liquid part of blood and is used in a variety of medical treatments and therapies. Plasma donation centers collect plasma from donors, who are compensated for their time and effort.

Plasma donation is generally safe and does not have any significant long-term health risks, as the body can regenerate plasma quickly. However, it is important to ensure that the donation center follows proper protocols and that the donor is in good health.

To start selling your plasma, you will need to find a reputable plasma donation center in your area. Many centers have websites where you can learn more about the donation process, eligibility requirements, and compensation rates.

Before donating plasma, it is important to follow the center's guidelines for preparation. This may include avoiding certain foods and beverages, as well as getting a good night's sleep. The actual donation process takes about an hour and involves the use of a sterile needle to collect the plasma. Here are some resources to help you find plasma donation centers and learn more about the process:

1. *Biolife Plasma Services* - Biolife has over 140 plasma donation centers across the United States. You can visit their website to find a location near you, schedule an appointment, and learn more about the donation process.
2. *CSL Plasma* - CSL Plasma has more than 270 plasma donation centers in the United States, Europe, and China. You can visit their website to find a location near you and learn more about the donation process.
3. *Octapharma Plasma* - Octapharma Plasma has more than 100 plasma donation centers in the United States. You can visit their website to find a location near you, schedule an appointment, and learn more about the donation process.

4. *Grifols Plasma* - Grifols Plasma has more than 250 plasma donation centers in the United States. You can visit their website to find a location near you and learn more about the donation process.

5. *Plasma Donation* - This website provides information on plasma donation centers in the United States, Canada, and Europe. You can search for a center by location and read reviews from other donors.

6. *DonatingPlasma.org* - This website is run by the Plasma Protein Therapeutics Association and provides information on plasma donation, including the benefits of plasma, what to expect during the donation process, and how to find a plasma donation center near you.

The amount of money that the average person can generate monthly selling plasma can vary depending on several factors such as the frequency of donation, location, and the individual plasma center's compensation rates. In the United States, plasma donors can typically earn between $20 to $50 per donation, with most centers allowing donors to donate twice a week. This means that if a person donates plasma twice a week, they can earn around $160 to $400 per month.

Before donating plasma, it's important to research the process and any potential risks or side effects. Make sure to also check the eligibility requirements for plasma donation, as they can vary depending on the donation center and your health status. Selling your plasma can be a way to generate passive income while helping those in need of plasma for medical purposes. However, it is important to carefully consider the risks and benefits, as well as to choose a reputable and safe plasma donation center.

Participate in Medical Studies

Participating in medical studies can be a way to earn passive income by offering your body as a subject for research in the medical field. Medical studies can range from testing new medications, evaluating the safety and efficacy of medical devices, or researching the impact of certain lifestyle choices on health outcomes.

One way to participate in medical studies is to register with a clinical research organization (CRO), which connects potential participants with relevant studies. Some CROs include Covance, Parexel, and PRA Health Sciences.

Another option is to look for opportunities at local research institutions, such as universities or hospitals, which may have ongoing studies in need of participants. These studies may be listed on their websites, or you can contact the institution's research department to inquire about potential opportunities.

It's important to note that participating in medical studies does come with some risks and potential side effects, so it's important to thoroughly read and understand the informed consent forms provided by the study organizers. It's also important to ensure that the study is being conducted by a reputable organization and that proper ethical guidelines are being followed.

Additionally, compensation for participating in medical studies can vary widely depending on the type and duration of the study, as well as the location and specific requirements of the study. Some studies may offer a one-time payment or stipend, while others may offer ongoing compensation for regular participation over an extended period.

There are several resources available to find medical studies that pay for participants. Here are some of them:

1. *ClinicalTrials.gov*: This is a database of clinical trials conducted worldwide. It is maintained by the National Institutes of Health

and provides information on the purpose of the study, eligibility criteria, location, and compensation.

2. ***ResearchMatch.org***: This is a free online registry that matches volunteers with clinical studies. It is maintained by the National Institutes of Health and provides information on the purpose of the study, eligibility criteria, location, and compensation.

3. ***CenterWatch.com***: This website provides information on clinical trials, including the purpose of the study, eligibility criteria, location, and compensation.

4. ***Craigslist.org***: This is a classifieds website that has a section for gigs and part-time jobs. Some medical studies pay for participants and may advertise on this site.

5. ***Local hospitals and clinics***: Hospitals and clinics in your area may conduct medical studies and may be looking for participants. You can contact them directly to inquire about opportunities.

The amount paid for participating in medical studies varies widely depending on the specific study, the length of time required, the location, and the type of study. Some studies may only pay a few hundred dollars, while others can pay several thousand dollars. It's important to note that participating in medical studies may involve certain risks and potential side effects, so it's important to carefully consider the risks and benefits before participating. It's also important to only participate in reputable studies conducted by qualified researchers and institutions.

It's important to note that participating in medical studies can come with potential risks and side effects, so it's important to carefully read and understand the informed consent form before participating. It's also a good idea to consult with your healthcare provider before participating in a study, and to only participate in studies that are being conducted ethically and with proper oversight.

Participate In Paid Online Surveys

Participating in paid online surveys is a great way to generate passive income. Companies and market research firms are always looking for feedback on their products and services, and they are willing to pay for your opinions. By sharing your thoughts and experiences, you can earn rewards such as cash, gift cards, or other prizes.

To get started with paid online surveys, you can sign up for survey websites that connect you with market research companies. Some of the top survey sites include *Swagbucks*, *Survey Junkie*, and *Vindale Research*. These sites offer a variety of surveys on different topics and typically pay between $0.50 to $5 per survey. You can also find focus groups and product testing opportunities on these sites, which typically pay more.

It's important to note that participating in online surveys will not make you rich overnight. However, it can be a great way to earn some extra cash in your free time. The key to success is to sign up for multiple survey sites and check your email regularly for survey invitations. You should also complete your profile and provide accurate and honest information to ensure that you qualify for as many surveys as possible.

Another thing to keep in mind is that some survey sites are more reputable than others. Before signing up, be sure to research the company and read reviews from other users to ensure that it's legitimate and pays out rewards as promised. You should also be cautious of any survey site that requires you to pay a fee to sign up or promises unrealistic earnings.

There are many resources available for finding paid online survey opportunities. Here are some options to consider:

1. Survey websites: There are numerous survey websites available that allow you to sign up and participate in surveys in exchange for payment. Some popular options include *Swagbucks*, *Survey Junkie*, and *Vindale Research*.
2. Market research companies: Many market research companies conduct surveys on behalf of their clients and pay participants for

their feedback. Some of the major companies in this space include **Ipsos**, **Nielsen**, and **Toluna**.

3. Online panels: Online panels are groups of people who have signed up to participate in surveys on a regular basis. Some of the top online panel providers include **Harris Poll Online**, **Pinecone Research**, and **American Consumer Opinion**.

4. Social media: Following social media accounts of survey websites and market research companies can be a good way to stay up to date on new survey opportunities. You can also join online communities focused on paid surveys, such as the **Reddit** subreddit **r/beermoney.**

5. Paid survey aggregators: These websites compile paid survey opportunities from multiple sources into one location. Examples include **SurveyPolice** and **PaidSurveys.net**.

When searching for paid online survey opportunities, it's important to be cautious and avoid any scams. Legitimate survey companies will not charge you to participate, so if a website is asking for payment or sensitive personal information, it's likely a scam. It's also a good idea to read reviews and do some research on a company before signing up to ensure they have a good reputation and pay participants on time.

If you're considering paid online surveys for passive income, here are some things to be aware of:

1. *Legitimacy*: Not all survey websites are legitimate, and some may be scams. Be sure to research the website or company before signing up and providing personal information.

2. *Time commitment*: While completing online surveys can be done in your free time, some surveys may take longer than others. Be aware of the time commitment involved and ensure that it's worth the potential payout.

3. *Payment methods*: Payment methods can vary between survey websites, with some offering cash payments while others offer gift cards or other rewards. Be aware of the payment methods and ensure that they're suitable for you.

4. *Eligibility*: Some surveys may have specific eligibility criteria, such as age, gender, or location. Be aware of these criteria and ensure that you're eligible to participate in the surveys.
5. *Survey frequency*: The frequency of available surveys can vary, with some websites offering more surveys than others. Be aware of the survey frequency and ensure that it's sufficient for your passive income goals.
6. *Privacy*: Be aware of the privacy policy of the survey website or company and ensure that your personal information is protected.
7. *Income potential*: Paid online surveys may not provide a substantial amount of passive income, and the potential earnings can vary depending on the website or company. Be realistic about the potential earnings and ensure that they align with your passive income goals.

The amount of money an average person can earn from participating in paid surveys varies depending on several factors, such as the number of surveys they complete, the length and complexity of the surveys, and the company offering the surveys.

Assuming a person completes several surveys per day and earns an average of $1 per survey, they could potentially earn anywhere from $30 to $90 per month. However, it's important to note that paid surveys are not a reliable source of income and may not be suitable for everyone.

Participating in paid online surveys can be a simple and easy way to generate passive income. While it may not make you rich, it can provide some extra cash in your pocket and the opportunity to share your opinions on products and services. Just be sure to sign up for reputable survey sites and provide honest feedback to ensure that you qualify for as many surveys as possible.

Conclusion

Thank you for reading *The Lazy Entrepreneur: 101 Passive Income Ideas Anyone Can Do*. This book aimed to inspire and guide individuals who aspire to generate passive income. By exploring 101 different ideas, we have shown that there are numerous opportunities to make money without having to actively trade your time for income. From renting out your attic to retail arbitrage, virtual real estate to raw land investments, the world of passive income is constantly evolving and offers something for everyone. As I wrap up this book, my last bit of advice is as follows:

1. *Stay persistent!* Generating passive income requires time, effort, and dedication. Don't get discouraged by setbacks and keep pushing forward until you achieve your financial goals.
2. *Keep learning!* The world of passive income is constantly evolving, so it's important to stay up to date with the latest trends, technologies, and strategies. Keep reading books, attending seminars, and networking with like-minded individuals to expand your knowledge and expertise.
3. *Be patient!* Building a sustainable passive income stream takes time, so be patient and focus on the long-term. Avoid get-rich-quick schemes and instead, invest in reliable and proven strategies that align with your goals and values.
4. *Don't forget to enjoy life!* While generating passive income is important, don't forget to enjoy life and pursue your passions. Balance your financial goals with your personal goals and prioritize your happiness and well-being above all else.
5. *Give back!* Finally, consider giving back to society and making a positive impact in the world. Use your passive income streams to support causes you believe in, volunteer your time and resources to help others, and contribute to making the world a better place.

With the right mindset, determination, and a willingness to learn, anyone can become a successful lazy entrepreneur and enjoy the freedom that passive income brings. So, start exploring, take action, and discover the power of generating passive income.